Finding Deep Joy

Finding Deep Joy

by

Robert Ellwood

Quest Books
Theosophical Publishing House

Wheaton, Illinois ♦ Chennai (Madras), India

The Theosophical Society wishes to acknowledge the generous support of the Kern Foundation in the publication of this book.

The Theosophical Publishing House
P. O. Box 270
Wheaton, Illinois 60189-0270

The images in this book appear by the courtesy of the following photographers and agencies:
Corbis, pp. 14, 120, 138
Dan Doolin, p. 68
Gary Elbert, p. 128
Stefan Jannides/Masterfile, p. 106
Douglas Kirkland, p. 114
Michael Macintyre/Hutchison Library, p. 40
Jan Phillips, pp. 2, 22, 32, 62, 92
Ron Sanford/International Stock, p. i

Library of Congress Cataloging-in-Publication Data

Ellwood, Robert S.
Finding deep joy / Robert Ellwood.-2nd Quest ed.
p. cm.
Includes bibliographical references.
ISBN 0-8356-0800-X
1. Spiritual life.   2. Joy-Religious aspects.   I. Title.

BL624.E46 2001
299'.934-dc21   2001041738

        5   4   3   2   1   *   01   02   03   04   05   06

Printed in the United States of America

Contents

Preface to the Second Edition   *vii*

Part One: *Exploring the Nature of Joy*

Chapter One: The Cosmic Dance   3

Chapter Two: The Morning Stars Singing Together   15

Chapter Three: Joy as Our Deepest Reality   23

Part Two: *Witnessing Joy*

Chapter Four: A Universe in Balance: Joy and Love   33

Chapter Five: Three Who Were Joyous   41

Part Three: *Discovering Joy for Ourselves*

Chapter Six: How Do We Begin?   63

Chapter Seven: A Spiritual Road Map   69

Part Four: *Living in Joy Every Day*

Chapter Eight: *Opening the Inner Doors*   93

Chapter Nine: *Creating a Lifestyle for Joy*   107

Chapter Ten: *For Richer for Poorer, in Sickness and in Health*   115

Chapter Eleven: *Living Fully in the Moment*   121

Chapter Twelve: *Transcending Obstacles*   129

Chapter Thirteen: *Finding Deep Joy Today*   139

Notes   143

Preface to the Second Edition

The second, revised edition of this book contains several new features, including illustrations and appropriate quotations in the page margins. At the end of each chapter a new section appears, "Entering into Joy," presenting examples from the spiritual lives of contemporary persons and suggesting exercises by which the reader might incorporate insights. The examples are generally culled from accounts written by my university students or by attendees at my lectures sponsored by the Theosophical Society in America. The writers have given consent for their use.

Preparing this new edition has been itself a joy, for the work has continually brought me closer to the ultimate wellsprings of human life and love. It is a book of which I feel unworthy, knowing all too well that I do not always dwell in its spiritual realm and that it is addressed as much to me as to anyone else. Yet preparing the book has doubtlessly extended my stays in that kingdom longer than would otherwise have been the case, and I can only trust and pray that my readers will be likewise blessed.

I would like to express my deep appreciation to Senior Editor Sharron Brown Dorr and other staff members of the Theosophical Publishing House; and to John Algeo, President of the Theosophical Society in America, for their generous advice and assistance in preparing this edition of *Finding Deep Joy*.

R. E.

Part One

Exploring
the
Nature of Joy

Chapter One

The
Cosmic Dance

*T*O THOSE WHO SEE ARIGHT, this vast and mysterious universe is as overflowing with joy as the old-fashioned heaven was overbursting with angels. Its stars throb with joy, its radiations hum with it, its dark or glowing nebulae embed it. The dances of the atoms and galaxies are dances of joy. Here below, joy lies hidden deep down at the heart of all things—boulders, trees, dolphins, zebras, and ourselves. Occasionally joy can be tapped in such a way that we can recognize its presence everywhere. It streams out of its secret places within us to flood the conscious mind with rapture keener than the sharpest grief and wider than any learning. I have experienced moments and hours when such joy has come to me, sometimes spontaneously and sometimes induced by meditation, for meditation seldom fails—sooner or later—to release the floodgates of joy and focus its dancing light.

In those moments, one is what life tends toward and what *being* is all about. These times of joy are not emotional quirks or manic moods; they are life supremely being itself, being what it wants to be, in touch with the being that is its true nature.

When this deep joy comes, it is just there, independent of outer events. It is entirely different from being happy *about* something, like getting a present or completing a successful business deal. It is a pure joy of *being* that can well up in the most ordinary settings, amid the drudgery of unglamorous work, or while drifting off to sleep, and it can come in meditation, even in a hospital bed or a prison cell.

The authenticity of these moments tells us that the universe, deep down, is joy, for at such times we feel closest to the universe and most a part of its material and spiritual nature. Joy is life realizing what its parent, the universe—God, if you wish—is, always was, and ever shall be.

I have known such joy, and there is certainly nothing about me, no special birth or virtue, that leads me to think I am any different from the rest of humanity. I am firmly convinced that this same joy is latent in all women and men; indeed, in all that is. It is in you!

As the true nature of life, joy can be touched and known by anyone, in whatever circumstances. In some people and places it may be near the surface, in others deeply buried. But if joy is the true stuff of the universe, there can be no place, however terrible, where its last glimmer has irretrievably flickered out.

I am led, then, to a wonderful faith—in itself a joy—that everyone can find and can know this deep joy. Joy is not only your right, your heritage; joy *is* you at the deepest level, and your joy is one with the infinite, timeless joy of the unbound universe. Find it and drink all you want of it—there's more than enough for all.

Yet so often we block deep joy. To block joy is our privilege as finite, particularized children of the universe, but it's an action hardly to our credit. We get caught up in our routines, our little fears and goals. We merely skim the surface of little puddles of joy as we run by, ignoring the vast oceans of it that wash up on the beach of our conscious minds. We may even think that, instead of joy, the untapped levels of mind are subcellars full of dirt and dragons. If only we knew—and we *can* know.

Our Shifting Moods

Take your average day. How many shifting moods and states of consciousness do you wend your way through before it's over?

You may wake up feeling logy, but you drag yourself out of bed. It's another day. Brushing teeth, getting dressed, putting on socks and shoes may be a little depressing, unless maybe you're wearing new clothes for the first time

*There was a jolly
    miller once
Lived on the River Dee
He worked and sang
    from morn till night
No lark more blithe
    than he.*
        —Isaac Bickerstaffe

or it's a very special day, like a child's Christmas or birthday. Otherwise, it's the same old thing over and over and over. The tedium of fixing and eating breakfast, perhaps the stress of getting children off to school may not be enjoyable either, but at least by now you're moving along with the clock.

If you like your job, you perk up by the time you get to work. Maybe you sense an honest flush of eager exhilaration as you walk into the office or shop, say "Good morning" all around, and get acquainted with that I've-got-a-job-to-do-and-a-place-in-the-world feeling.

But let's not forget the ups and downs at work. There's that other person in the shop who just can't seem to keep from rubbing you the wrong way, generating irritation—even anger. Or perhaps you feel frustration—a word we use a lot these days—with the letter that has to be rewritten twice and the important call to someone who seems always to have just stepped out or is still having lunch at three o'clock.

Still, there are good things: a breakthrough, that certain smile from someone special, the simple low-key but steady satisfaction of doing a job well. Then, during a lunch break or on the way home, something makes the world stop and stabs you with wonder—a V-shaped flight of wild geese winging as though late for an appointment at the edge of the earth; or at dusk, the light cast by a silver moon just past full. Finally, the day ends with a good book in front of the fire or quiet chuckling at a TV comedy.

Or it could be the other way around. You're one of those people who wake full of zeal and sparkle and get a lot

High above the city
Dawn flares
From a window-washer's
*   pail.*
*   —Cor van den Heuvel*

done even before breakfast. But you run out of steam before the day does. You wander around zombie-like, tired and depressed with evening chores, until you can drop into bed.

The world is divided into morning people and night people. Either way, your day is a kaleidoscope of states of consciousness and shifting moods. Your feelings, even of who you are, do not stay the same. You probably roam through dozens of states of thought and feeling, ranging from intense concentration to lethargy and depression to exuberant happiness to high spiritual joy. Sometimes you shift from one to another for no apparent reason, and you wonder why.

It could be that a natural law of compensation is at work here. Just as summer shifts to winter or a fire burns itself out and turns to cold ash, one feeling gives way to another. After doing hard, concentrated work for a while, you have a real need to take a break, put your mind in low gear, and get a drink or gaze out the window.

Similarly, after going through a great personal joy or sorrow—falling in love or losing a loved one—you come to a point where you just don't feel it so strongly anymore. You may even feel emotionally numb. When the original intensity of joy or sorrow fades, you may wonder if something is wrong. Don't I really love my lover? Am I not truly grieved over this loss? In the case of a powerful religious experience, a born-again conversion, or a mystical exaltation, you may wonder in the light of common day if you have committed some great sin that caused God to withdraw his presence.

Some people do not fully understand that these changes in state of mind and feeling are natural. You may

So on we worked and waited for the light.
—Edwin Arlington Robinson

The universe is change;
our life is what our
thoughts make it.
　　　—Marcus Aurelius

The Master said,
A knight whose heart
is set upon the Way,
but who is ashamed of
wearing shabby clothes
and eating coarse food
is not worth calling
into counsel.
*—***The Analects of Confucius**

even worry or feel guilty about them. At such times, the fact of the love or loss or conversion is still there, but the feelings have shifted toward neutral to rest up for the next big event. They are taking a much-needed break, as natural as a break from any strenuous work or the alternation of sleep and waking. In fact, maintaining the same mood all the time can be a sign of serious mental illness. The person who is always giddily high or deeply depressed has real problems and needs help.

This is how normal life works. It is a play back and forth of ordinary moods and feelings, affected by outside events and natural inner rhythms. You're happy when good things happen and unhappy when bad things come. You're also up and down in response to biological patterns of energy and depletion and because of the natural ebb and flow of consciousness.

When happiness arises on this level, it is basically a reactive response to stimuli or rhythms, like waves cresting on the sea in response to wind and tides. You can try to strengthen the pattern by making good things happen as much as possible and controlling the downs chemically and otherwise. Still, it's like being in a rowboat on a rough sea.

The outer world constantly bombards us with appeals to find happiness through manipulations of our environment, especially in ways that keep the material economy rolling. Buy this product, have this experience, go here or there, move to another job, be fulfilled in one way or another. All such appeals are part of a consumer society and play the necessary role of making jobs and helping society work.

However, these manipulations can end in misery when they encourage us to think that happiness is merely a matter of having and doing the right stuff. No matter how much you have, you are still subject to natural shifts in the spectrum of consciousness and to natural limitations. Not everyone can own all that the ads dangle in front of us; not everyone can be as gorgeous as the media models; not everyone—even in an affluent society—will have the good life depicted by the tube and popular magazines.

If your happiness depends on such dreams, you are bound to be finally disappointed. You will find that life turns into nothing more than a great weariness and a great emptiness. Even getting what you thought you wanted does not deliver all it seems to promise, or if it does bring some happiness, what you want soon changes to something else. Above all, questing for happiness in the world of things turns our gaze away from the genuine wellsprings of deep joy, which have little to do with possessions, excitement, entertainment, or fun—though deep joy enhances all innocent pleasure.

Joyful Abundance

All of us can discover and tap into a depth of joy far beneath the level of happiness. Such joy is like the deep still sea miles under the rise and fall of waves, the universal joy of joy itself.

That joy is what this book is about. What I want to share with you is the realization that true joy is not just

Yield and overcome;
Bend and be straight;
Empty and be full;
Wear out and be new;
Have little and gain;
Have much and be
   confused . . .

Be really whole,
And all things will come
   to you.
   —The Tao Te Ching *of*
      Lao Tzu

page 9

another feeling among many that come and go. It is the deepest, most fundamental reality of the universe. It is of a different order than sorrow or lethargy or ordinary happiness.

These emotions may seem to trade places as equals with real joy from time to time, but that sense is illusory. Clouds sometimes obscure the sun, but they are hardly equal to it. Clouds come and go, while the sun is there all the time, even when its light is momentarily hidden. Indeed, the sun is many, many times bigger than the whole earth upon which the clouds are themselves but fleeting mists, and it was there long before the earth coalesced and cooled and the very first mists arose.

Joy is the most basic reality of the universe and of ourselves as parts of it: to seek this joy above all else is not a selfish quest. Living for sensual pleasure and ordinary happiness may indeed be selfish if pursued without thought for others, but the joy of the universe operates by very different laws. The more of this joy you have, the more others have, too, for it is inevitably shared. The more joy you give, the more sensitive you are to the blockage of joy in others, and the more you are drawn through love to help them find joy. Ordinary happiness wants to get; joy wants to give.

The primacy of joy is clearly expressed in the world's great spiritual traditions, which promise joy in this life and the life to come for those who live in accordance with the will of God; that is, with the real nature of things. Religions generally portray the saint or enlightened being as a person of supremely deep joy, suggested by the aureole or halo.

For example, the Upanishads, the most philosophical of the Vedic scriptures of ancient India, tell us that Brahman

You must become an ignorant man again And see the sun again with an ignorant eye.
—Wallace Stevens

(God) is joy: "For from joy all beings are born, by joy they are sustained, being born, and into joy they enter after death."[1] The same passage tells us that Brahman is also food, energy, mind, and intellect, but the deepest truth is that Brahman is joy. Brahman, though one, is all things, as a single flame takes many different shapes. But it is not Brahman's conditioned existence as the multiplicity of things that is the fullness of joy. Rather, Brahman as infinite reality pours endless depths into each conditioned experience, which makes it possible for all to be flooded with deep joy. As the Upanishads say elsewhere, "Only in the Infinite is there joy." And as a commentator on the Vedas said, "[T]he universe, with everything in it, is only an outward flow and a crystallized form of the unceasingly upwelling Joy of Brahman."[2]

If this declaration is true, then we ought to be able to know joy in each moment, in each person we meet, or each object we see, however transitory the event, unprepossessing the person, or trivial the object to the casual eye. For behind it—or behind him or her—is the infinite joyousness of the universe.

Truly I tell you, just as you did it to one of the least of these my brothers, you did it to me.

—Jesus, in Matt. 25:40

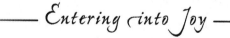

Entering into Joy

Others have described their moments of deepest joy this way:

In the early, early morning, before any clutter enters my mind

Chapter One

When I am in nature and feel at one with a leaf or a blade of grass

When I'm being creative in placing objects so that they are aesthetically pleasing

When I'm doing a good job, feeling competent, even expert, at times

Connecting with the right person at the right time

Pausing during a hectic workday to enjoy the blue sky and say, "Thank you"

Listening to the birds or the laughter of children

When I'm spending time with the wise elderly woman who lives down the street

Sitting on my porch watching the sunset

When I'm playing hide-and-seek in the dark with my grandson

In the midst of good friends

Feeling that I truly understand and have been understood by someone I care about

Dancing

Think back over your life and record the moments when you have felt the most joy. Perhaps they have occurred while singing, or sitting by the ocean, or holding a child for the first time. Perhaps they have to do with the smell of autumn, or reunions with loved ones, or the satisfaction of having helped someone. Consider keeping a journal for this purpose. That way, you can begin to identify patterns of experiences that bring you joy, which may help you increase them.

The Cosmic Dance

Try this simple exercise: Without staring, but with gentle focus, look at a sleeping pet, a room full of fun projects, a tree, a door, a flower, or the face—and especially the eyes—of someone you love. Sit quietly, looking at your chosen image until you know its joy.

Chapter Two

The Morning Stars Singing Together

ONE OF THE MOST PROFOUND books in the Judeo-Christian Bible is the Book of Job. Job, the protagonist, is a man of great piety and prosperity, a sublime example of the good person duly rewarded. But Satan challenges God, saying that if he takes everything away from Job, Job will curse God. So is it done. Job loses his property, his children die, and he is afflicted from head to foot with painful boils.

His wife tells him to curse God and die, but Job will curse only the day of his birth. "Let the day perish in which I was born, and the night that said, 'A man-child is conceived.'" He neither curses nor forgives God, but understandably complains that in no way does he deserve such suffering; he questions whether a God that allows it can be called "good" or "just." Or, if God is good, his power must be limited; the bad things that happen are outside his control. Job lapses into despair over such thoughts.

What, finally, can be more immeasurably depressing than a gnawing suspicion—or conviction—that the universe is without control or moral order—its God, if there is one, either a divine weakling or less good than we, his subjects, at our best. Job laments: "Every terror that haunted me has caught up with me, and all that I feared has come upon me. There is no peace of mind nor quiet for me; I chafe in torment and have no rest" (Job 3:25, 26).[3]

Job is then visited by three friends who, like well-meaning friends in all ages, try to make him feel better by assuring him that a just and loving God is in charge, who indeed causes the righteous to prosper and sinners to suffer. Job must be guilty enough, they say, to render this punishment just, for all men are sinners; it is pretentious to claim otherwise. But Job cannot accept that somehow he deserves his afflictions.

He knows he has not sinned, at least in proportion to his present woe; nor did his innocent but dead children, and he will not save God's reputation by saying he did. So desperate is our yearning for a just universe that we are often tempted to cheat and see the sweet and sour of life distributed more even-handedly than honesty allows. Job refuses to do so. He knows the conventional pieties of his companions do not hold up, and he is too honest to pretend

Shall we receive the good at the hand of God, and not receive the bad?
—Job 2:9–10

Amid thoughts from visions of the night, when deep sleep falls on mortals, Dread came upon me, and trembling, Which made all my bones shake.
—Job 4:13–14

otherwise. Nor does he curse God outright, for he believes God does send good as well as ill. But he takes God to task for his own woes, which seem to mock God's pretensions to justice and mercy.

Then comes the famous scene in which God, responding to Job, questions him from the whirlwind. "Where were you," inquires the Lord, "when I laid the earth's foundations, when I measured out the dimensions of creation, when the morning stars sang together, and all the sons of God shouted aloud?" (Job 38:7)

This passage and the magnificent description of the wonders of creation surpassing human understanding that follow have been subject to many interpretations. To me, it seems that an underlying theme of God's response to Job is identical to the theme of this book: joy.

The universe as God made it is permeated with splendor and exuberance, full of wondrous vitality, clearly alive with the thrill of being. Against that whirlwind of light and life, Job's injustices, while not denied, are put in perspective.

Individual lives, both human and animal, come and go; stars and even systems of stars have their cycles of birth and death over unimaginable eons, yet the joyous process of creation goes on and on. Even while we, on the human scale of experience, may lament real evil, the atoms and molecules within our bodies continue their wheeling dances as though ecstatic with rapture, and so does the spinning planet upon which we sit.

So long as Job sees himself as distinct from the deep joy and wonder all around and within him, he will never find satisfaction, for without participating in that great

If I sin, what do I do to you, you watcher of humanity? Why have you made me your target? Why have I become a burden to you?

—Job 7:20

page 17

dance he is incomplete. Joining it in spirit, he will find a joy deeper than any sorrow. He does find that joy—through grasping wonder far greater than himself, as suggested by his final response to God:

But I have spoken of great things...too wonderful for me to know. I knew of thee then only by report, but now I see thee with my own eyes. Therefore I melt away (Job 42:3–6).

For hatred does not cease by hatred at any time: hatred ceases by love— this is the eternal law.
—The Dhammapada
(Buddhist text)

These words do not mean that the injustices of the world are of no consequence, that we have no calling to struggle against them or to help the innocent victims of natural or human violence. To take that attitude would be to deny compassion. Love or compassion is the supreme ethical value simply because it expresses the unity of the universe. Love is the drive that wants to bring people and things together, and so it is the drive in accordance with the real nature of the universe—oneness. Its opposite, hatred, which wants to alienate and separate and distance people and things, is at cross-purposes with the true nature of the universe and so can never ultimately prevail. The unity and joy of the universe are inseparable, and compassion as the true way of life is inseparable from them.

Hence, compassion is simply expressing in action the interrelatedness of all life, all being; the person who talks about cosmic oneness but does not express it in compassion has not begun to understand it. Note that part of Job's reconciliation was that he prayed for the very friends who had given him poor advice. "The Lord showed favor to Job when he had interceded for his friends" (Job 42:9).

Living in Joy No Matter What

Deep joy is both the ground of love and the surest source of strength to persevere in the course of compassion—even when trials abound, as they often will. For joy and love in this world often find themselves set amid neighbors of very different stripe. The great Buddhist classic, the Dhammapada, tells us that if we live close to our own inner sources, we can abide in joy regardless of outer conditions.

> Live in joy,
> In love,
> Even among those who hate.
>
> Live in joy,
> In health,
> Even among the afflicted.
>
> Live in joy,
> In Peace,
> Even among the troubled.
>
> Live in joy,
> Without possessions,
> Like the shining ones . . .
>
> Look within.
> Be still. Free from fear and attachment,
> Know the sweet joy of the way.[4]

The premise, again, is that a substratum of deep joy underlies all of life and consciousness. Life and consciousness *are* joy in their pure form; all else are wind and rocks that tumble joy around, just as the ocean is water in which waves may rise and fall, in which rocks may intrude and "winds their revels keep."

We may be so busy riding the waves that we little remember what the waves themselves are made of. We may get so lost in the ups and downs of life that we forget what life itself is—the sheer joyousness of energy, of being alive, of pure consciousness—that is, pure joy consciousness before it is modified to become consciousness of anything.

Entering into Joy

Here is a graduate student's paraphrased story:

When my mother was having a hard time getting sober, I started going to Alcoholics Anonymous with her. I loved these meetings, which were better than church. Everyone shared his or her own experience. They were all different kinds of people, from doctors to housewives, but most had been stripped of everything. Some had been in the gutter, close to death; some had the DTs, some had been incarcerated.

But here they became wonderfully spiritual and shared their stories with such love that the whole room would vibrate. Here was affirmation, support, and nonjudgmentalism. These people knew the only way to stay sober was to be honest. As I heard my mother speak about her own life, I began to accept her and to see her in a different light. I felt proud of her and came away feeling reinforced.

Pain, disappointment, suffering, and death are realities in everyone's life. Think about your own greatest heartaches and hardships. Then consider what the God who spoke to Job out of the whirlwind would say about them. What can you affirm of value beyond these painful experiences? What can you affirm of value in them?

Whatever your present circumstances, list ten things for which you are grateful today. They can be as simple as the sound of birdsong, the feel of the sun on your face, a meal well made, or a phone call from a friend.

Chapter Three

Joy as Our Deepest Reality

LIFE AND MIND ARE JOY *embodied*. In this state joy may be more vulnerable than before, but it is still joy above all. The Vedanta philosophical tradition, based on the Upanishads, speaks of Brahman as *sat-chit-ananda*—being, knowledge, bliss, or joy. This joy is primordial reality, the horizonless sea on which we are each a cresting wave, taking transitory shape, but of the same stuff as the profoundest depths.

So it is that the Upanishads relate that Brahman, being-knowledge-joy, is the Atman or soul, the innermost nature, of all beings, ourselves included. All else is superimposed upon that fundamental essence. Surrounding the Atman of each of us as a human being are five "sheaths" or aspects of human nature. Each draws power from the preceding one, which is closer to the Atman, and then expresses the Atman-reality in a more outward and conditioned way.

The innermost sheath (next to the Atman itself and expressing its deepest nature) is *ananda*, JOY! Our deepest nature as selves, as well as the quintessential nature of God, is JOY!

Moving outward from joy is spiritual insight (*buddhi*)— the flash of true intellect that borrows its spark from the inward joy of being and expresses it in the radiant but still more conditioned form of intellectual creativity.

Next after insight is mind (*manas*), in the lower sense of memory and the routine mental functions. Mind seizes its sparkle from insight and expresses thought in the mundane tasks of storing insight in memory and attending to the ordinary tasks of life. Even so, joy can spring from within.

After mind is life energy (*prana*) and finally the physical form (*rupa*), which provides a vehicle for the whole range of human capacities.

According to this model, as you work or play or walk down the street, essentially you *are* the Atman—God, Brahman, the Essence of the Universe—replete with being-knowledge-joy, birthless and deathless, unconditioned by space, time, or motion. You are a role the universe is playing, and you are also the One who is playing this and all other roles. You are one—and *the* One—of whom the

Joy as Our Deepest Reality

Upanishads say:

O Brahman Supreme!
Formless art thou, and yet
(Though the reason none knows)
Thou bringest forth many forms;
Thou bringest them forth, and then
Withdrawest them to thyself.
Fill us with thoughts of thee!

Thou art the fire,
Thou art the sun,
Thou art the air,
Thou art the moon,
Thou art the starry firmament,
Thou art Brahman Supreme:
Thou art the waters—thou,
The creator of all!

Thou art woman, thou art man,
Thou art the youth, thou art the maiden,
Thou art the old man tottering with his staff;
Thou facest everywhere.

Thou art the dark butterfly,
Thou art the green parrot with red eyes,
Thou art the thunder cloud, the seasons, the seas.
Without beginning art thou,
Beyond time, beyond space,
Thou art he from whom sprang
The three worlds.

Forgetting and Remembering

Each of us is a form of the divine dance, yet we forget our original nature. Our world is like a drama, a play on a wide stage, that has been going on for ages. It has been playing so long that the actors have forgotten they are acting and completely identify with their parts. They are in anguish when another character in the play is killed, thinking that person really dead. When loves are sealed and broken, the actors as lovers live out the scene as though it were their only life. Finally, the prompters behind the scenes must remind them that, in the words of Shakespeare:

> All the world's a stage,
> And all the men and women merely players:
> They have their exits and their entrances;
> And one man in his time plays many parts.[5]

Indeed, from the perspective of full being, knowledge, and joy, there is a real sense in which, in the words of the Bard elsewhere:

> These our actors . . . were all spirits, and
> Are melted into air, into thin air;
> And, like the baseless fabric of this vision,
> The cloud-capp'd towers, the gorgeous palaces,
> The solemn temples, the great globe itself,
> Yea, all which it inherit shall dissolve
> And, like this insubstantial pageant faded,

An empty elevator
opens
closes
— *Jack Cain*

The circus tent
all folded up:
October mist . . .
— *Eric Amann*

Joy as Our Deepest Reality

Leave not a rack behind. We are such stuff
As dreams are made.[6]

From the Vedanta point of view, the world, though it has its own kind of reality, exists for the actors caught in it only because they accept its reality and act accordingly. But in Vedanta there is finally but one actor, Brahman, who animates all the parts, though our separate conscious minds usually overidentify with the parts we play. Nevertheless, we can be recalled to our true identity.

How do we identify with the drama? Let us look at it in terms of the five aspects of human nature mentioned in the last chapter, beginning with the innermost. These events do not necessarily occur in temporal sequence, at least on the level of ordinary time as we experience it. But it is helpful to think of our separation from the One and identification with the drama of the many as a linear process.

The first stage, *ananda*, bliss, is very subtle: a separate joy. God experiences the joy of which divinity is comprised as both one and infinitely many. Joy wants to see, to know, and to play; and for these pleasures, it requires that which is other than itself. Hence, it knows itself as both one and as individuated, just as within the infinite sea of divine joy, frolicking waves rise and break into foam.

Joy is creative, and creativity is the seeking and making of meaningful relationships. Not only does the playfulness of joy require that it experience separateness, but in its creativity it also seeks to unite. It is seeing and using things in more than just a separative way: it is relating to them, participating with them. Joy, then, first expresses insight, for

Everyone and everything around me takes on the feeling of having been there always . . . We are sitting in a garden . . . of fuchsias and humming-birds in a valley that leads down to the westernmost ocean, and where the gulls take refuge in storms . . . And yet we seem to have been there forever.

—Alan Watts

insight is the power of creative mind that sees and intellectually makes connections.

The second stage, *buddhi*, insight, requires support in its own patterns—its memory banks, routine responses to stimuli, and times of low-level functioning. It cannot always operate on the high plane of flashing creativity, so it expresses itself in the lower mind.

The third level, *manas*, ordinary mind, is a particularized, individualized person. While ultimately entities may inhere in the same joy, they will not have exactly the same ideas, memories, emotions, problems, or responses. An individual needs something to run on in this world where joy has become congealed into mind and light frozen into matter.

The fourth level, then, is *prana*, life energy. There is a fifth, *rupa*, the physical form that provides the energized vehicle for what began as a separate joy.

You can experience this process in reverse. Starting with awareness of the body, you can inwardly explore yourself step by step, acquainting yourself fully with each more inward aspect in turn. You can discover how each works and relates to the others until you have arrived at deep joy and the Atman, which in itself is nonindividualized and which underlies them all. There you can express reality bare, beside which the drama enacted through the individualized self is only an insubstantial pageant. Turning outward again, you will reenter your role with a renewed spirit of joy and playfulness.

I have merged, like the bird, with the bright air, And my thought flies to the place by the bo-tree. Being, not doing, is my first joy.
—*Theodore Roethke*

— Entering into Joy —

These occasions of deep joy, from the suggestions of real people, suggest the five sheaths of being:

- *Dancing (rupa: physical form)*
- *Being in a flower garden (prana: life energy and sense awareness)*
- *Appreciating old friends (manas: memory and mind)*
- *Following one's inner voice (buddhi: insight and creative intellect)*
- *Laughing spontaneously (ananda: our deepest nature—JOY!)*

How are you most aware of these five sheaths in your own life? How, in different situations, do you experience your physical body, your vital energy, your mind, your intuition, and your sense of the Divine within? What experiences might you seek to bring your life more into balance?

Part Two

Witnessing Joy

Chapter Four

A Universe in Balance: Joy and Love

CAN WE REALLY BE SURE that joy is the most basic reality in the universe and in ourselves? Here are some further considerations.

1. Joy represents a state of equilibrium, one that is tension free. All entities in the universe, living or nonliving, move to relieve tension and attain equilibrium. In sentient beings, joy is the feeling that wells up when this goal is attained; as a goal, joy can be thought of as the absolute to which all else is process, moving toward it and so dependent upon it.

Planets circle their star in response to the tension between their inertial energy and the star's gravitational pull. Animals seek to satisfy their hunger and thirst. We endure the psychological tension of a long day's work with thoughts of a relaxing evening or summer vacation. (But often these dreams lead to frantic searches for diversion rather than tapping into the deep joy that is already present at all times and in all places.)

2. That we are capable of joy means that a potential for joy exists—as a potential for consciousness must exist—embedded in the very nature of the universe. We have no need or right to think of ourselves, with our consciousness and capabilities for joy, as freaks who somehow got caught in this universe, but who, except for our physical nature, have nothing in common with it.

True, much modern science assumes that all those unimaginably deep reaches of space strewn with the dust of galaxies contain almost nothing but inert matter, forming and reforming in accordance with blind physical law. This view makes the mind behind the eyes peering through the telescope a strange outsider to the show. Such a mind must somehow have either dropped from another sphere or inexplicably emerged in a universe essentially alien to consciousness. If so, why are we here at all?

It would make more sense to recognize that, because our atoms and molecules have organized themselves in a way that enables consciousness to express itself, a potential for consciousness lurks in every atom of the universe. And if consciousness, then also joy, for joy is built into consciousness as that toward which all its movements tend, as

But each creature turneth round on itself, as a wheel doth, and turneth in such a way as to come back to its starting point.
—*Boethius*

Feeling like exiles undermines our incentive to change our perspective . . . As exiles, we have no responsibility, no choice; our free will is a mirage.
—*Amit Goswami*

that which sweeps over it when its tensions are relieved and its natural equilibrium is established.

3. Joy—or something like it—must pervade the vast universe as a whole. The wheeling of planets around the sun, the rush of galaxies over the horizon of visible space and time, and the spin of electrons all seem like the joy we feel when we whirl around at the behest of natural forces—swinging, diving, riding a merry-go-round. These are not occasions of tension but of deep release, of equilibrium, of exciting vertigo. They are play—play *is* moving equilibrium, and in it joy wells up. Play is active joy.

How much such thoughts about stars and electrons represent excessive anthropomorphizing no one can say. The sort of tension that can arise between our individualized consciousness and natural forces, or between two individualized consciousnesses, is not measurable by physics and astronomy. But if even a shimmer of consciousness—and therefore joy—glows in the universe from which we have risen, these comparisons are not wholly out of line. The universe, going down its invisible pathways through space and time, seems to be at play, acting out a game eons long, and so to have all the conditions we would associate with a joy so large and deep it is beyond our comprehension.

4. In another sense joy, like the universe, is timeless. We might think of time as we experience it psychologically as a function of the mind yearning for joy. We often comment that moments or hours of deep joy seem timeless—we don't know how long they last and it doesn't matter. Clock time goes fast or slow with little relation to time as we feel it. The eternal now that we sense is both older and

We have developed a science—idealist science—that is truly integrated within a spiritual philosophy of joy.
—Amit Goswami

When I was a child, all appeared new, and strange at first, inexpressible rare and delightful and beautiful . . . Boys and girls tumbling in the street, and playing, were moving jewels. I knew not that they were born or should die; but all things abided eternally as they were in their proper places. Eternity was manifest in the Light of the Day, and something infinite behind everything appeared.
—Thomas Traherne

"*Time*" *is only an illusion produced by the succession of our states of consciousness as we travel through Eternal Duration.*

—*H. P. Blavatsky*

Man is unhappy because he doesn't know he's happy.

—*Kirilov, in Dostoyevsky's* **The Possessed**

fresher than the granular dry time of ordinary workaday life. At such timeless moments we sense that the joy that creates them must also be a basic realty, more basic even than time measured by the stars in their courses.

5. Evil, including pain, is the opposite of joy, and often it seems to be just as real and even more powerful than joy. A moment of joy is strong—but joy as a presence in this hard world often seems fragile and fleeting. Can we honestly say that joy is more basic than evil?

Evil depends on one's scale, one's perspective. No discernible trace of it lies in the age-long dance of the atoms or in the play of the planets and galaxies. Awareness of evil exists only where life and consciousness, and so joy *as potential only*, are temporarily individualized, as in ourselves. The older and deeper all-pervading joy is still there on all the other scales, even when evil or pain are being endured at the level of consciousness controlled by individualized existence. Joy is always present in the atoms and molecules making up the flesh and blood of the sufferer, in the swing of the planet on which he or she stands, in the sun that gives warmth and life, and in the mighty dances of the universe. It exists on every scale other than that of personal consciousness and can always be tapped, even in the darkest suffering.

If these considerations are not enough to persuade us that joy is at the center of the universe and not just of human aspiration, reflect on the thought that joy has the basic characteristic of any center—it unites all the rest. Joy is unitive. It is when we are joyous that we are most united to others and to the universe. When in a joyful state of mind we look at a star, a rabbit, a tree, we feel part of the object, part of a system that embraces both it and ourselves and has joy as its ground.

Closely allied to joy is love. When we suffer, tension, fear, loneliness, and pain take over and separate us from joy. But with love, suffering can be overcome and incorporated into the system of joy. Both love and joy unite; both take delight in the other person or object.

Joy simply is; love is empathetic and can share pain as well as joy. Yet joy is the ground of love, for love is learned through fleeting awareness of the joy of perfect union. It bears even pain in order to restore that union and finds its strength in the ultimate joyous oneness of the universe.

The human love for which we quest all our lives is probably first learned from the infantile experience of symbiotic closeness to parents, especially nursing at the mother's breast. That primal experience indelibly imprints on us the union of love and joy; it tells us what is supremely desirable. Yet this humanized joy is based on the joy of the universe as a whole uniting all its parts, for the universe was there as a unity long before mother or child.

As we have seen, joy is also closely linked to creativity, for creating is also unitive; it is a form of love and so an expression of underlying joy. One who creates simply unites different elements in a new way, whether words in a poem, colors in a picture, plants in a garden, or ingredients in a meal.

The greatest creative work of joy aligned with love is the shaping of human lives. In many lives the search for joy is a hard one, but there are those who have sought joy and

Also he showed me a little thing, the quantity of a hazel-nut, in the palm of my hand . . . I marvelled how it might last . . . [a]nd was answered in my understanding: It lasteth, and ever shall last, for that God loveth it.

—Julian of Norwich

found it. They have found joy in themselves and in the universe, and they have found it in the infinite, in the supreme focus of love we call God. In our own pilgrimage toward joy, then, let us now turn to the lives of some who were joyous.

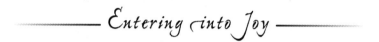

Entering into Joy

1) When in your life has joy most been aligned with love? Sit quietly and visualize that moment and the person who inspired it. If you feel led to do so, write a poem or draw a picture or find some other way to express the occasion.

2) Here a female Muslim student describes a remarkable experience that led to a fluid change of mood and appreciation of God:

I was in my home and under a great deal of stress. I was in a complete state of worry because I had lost a library book. I hadn't been able to find it for some weeks and was going to have to pay one hundred dollars for it. I was about twelve years old at the time, and it was a great deal of money. My mother was yelling at me frantically. I bent my head to pray and plead to God to help me find the book. When I raised my head up, as if toward the heavens, in front of me I saw the book! I felt so elated and overjoyed and touched by God himself. I felt so much love for Him and joyousness over what I thought at the time was a miracle.

In your own life, perhaps some hours, days, and even weeks seem like times of weaving back and forth between

Without this playing with fantasy no creative work has ever yet come to birth.
—C. G. Jung

extremes. Are you experiencing such a time right now? Hold the two extremes together in your mind until they come into balance.

Chapter Five

Three Who Were Joyous

I WANT TO INTRODUCE three saints of different religions who were particularly noted for bright joyousness of spirit. They are Rabi'a, the female Muslim Sufi poet/mystic; Pu Tai, the Chinese Buddhist monk who was the original of the well-known fat-bellied "laughing Buddha" of popular Chinese art; and St. Seraphim of Sarov, the celebrated Russian Orthodox lover of God.

At the outset, let us note that the joy of a saint can be a complex quality. It can be mixed with passionate yearning toward God, deep sorrow over sin, and hours of darkness

For me to be a saint means to be myself. Therefore the problem of sanctity and salvation is in fact the problem of finding out who I am and of discovering my true self.
—Thomas Merton

What is divine is the deep, interior source of acts, not the acts themselves. On the surface, there is nothing divine about nursing the sick, peeling carrots, or even praying.
—Bernadette Roberts

and despair when God seems to have hidden his face. Great saints do not function on a constant high pitch of rapture anymore than the rest of us. Indeed, what is great about the great saints, when their lives can be known and studied without the embellishment of legend and idealization, is that they were people who were great lovers of God and the world, despite a full share of human problems and weaknesses. If they were not like us, they could be of little relevance to our struggles. At the same time, their greatness shows us to what heights we can aspire.

We will, then, find in the lives of these saints times of difficulty and moments of sadness. But in these persons sorrow is intermingled with something else—a joy that does not suppress sorrow but goes deeper, sets limits to it, conditions it, and rides it out till joy breaks through and suffuses life again, like water covering the sea. We can understand this contradictory mixture of divine joy, human hardship, frustrated yearning, and despair of the lover of God, for our own joys are not always simple either.

The saint's combined joy and despair are like the feeling of a lover separated from the beloved or a parent from a child: at one and the same time there is joy in the love, in every thought of the other's face, yet sadness together with wistful yearning for an end to the separation. It is like the feelings we have when we strive to achieve a difficult goal, such as getting a coveted academic degree. Sometimes we feel a pleasant excitement at the challenge and enjoy wonderful moments of planning and dreaming. At other times the course may seem so hard that we give in to profound frustration or even despair. Yet deep down the joy is still there, because it is what makes us finally pull ourselves together and keep on. So it was with saints reaching for the Beloved, for God, at once higher than the highest heaven and nearer than hands and feet. Their goal was knowing and loving God perfectly, a goal constantly smiling at them through all events, yet at the end of a trail as infinitely long as God himself is deep.

A Transcendent Lover

God may do something silly at any time, because, like any lover, God does not reason. God is drunk with love.
—Ernesto Cardenal

In the eighth century after Christ and the second century after the prophet Muhammad, there lived in the city of Basra, in what is now Iraq, a woman called Rabi'a. She was orphaned as a child and made a slave who served her master by playing the flute. But that master, catching her at prayer, was impressed with her spirituality, so he gave her freedom.

Rabi'a spent the rest of her long life in poverty as a mystic lover of God, surrounded by spiritual friends and disciples. She was among the first of the Muslim mystics known as Sufis, and her example gave impetus to that movement, which was concerned with finding an inner intimacy with God beneath the externals of Islam. In Rabi'a's day the new faith had already swept across the Middle East, and she embraced it. Like the Sufis generally, she believed above all in loving God for his own sake, not for hope of reward or fear of hell, and in knowing him directly, not just on the authority of Muhammad or the Holy Koran. She once said, "I saw the Prophet in a dream, and he said to me,

'O Rabi'a, does thou love me?' I said, 'O Prophet of God, who is there who does not love thee? But my love to God has so possessed me that no place remains for loving or hating any save Him.'"[7] She also said, "O my Lord, if I worship Thee from fear of Hell, burn me in Hell, and if I worship Thee from hope of Paradise, exclude me thence, but if I worship Thee for Thine own sake then withhold not from me Thine Eternal Beauty."[8]

Rabi'a clearly distinguished two loves of God: that which worshipped him out of some separate motive, whether the authority of tradition and community or personal desire for heaven; and that which worshipped him for his own sake because he is the supreme object of human longing and love and the source of eternal joy. Rabi'a herself adored God for himself alone, and this was a deep and intimate matter, an affair between two passionate lovers.

At night Rabi'a would go up to her roof and pray, "O my Lord, the stars are shining and the eyes of men are closed, and kings have shut their doors, and every lover is alone with his beloved, and here am I alone with Thee."[9]

This deep love of God was generally expressed outwardly in a calm and joyous life. For Rabi'a, awareness of God in all his glory did not call for despair about the sin that separates us from God, for despair itself is an evil temptation. Though sin might drive her to tears, they were not tears of abject despair but part of the intricate spectrum of feelings proper to any love, through which she would better come to know the beloved and the complexities of relationship with him.

The soul is the secret chamber to which only God has the key. And if God does not enter, it remains empty.

—*Ernesto Cardenal*

Three Who Were Joyous

In her town dwelt another saint, Hasan of Basra. He was a holy man of the gloomiest sort, though an eloquent preacher and learned theologian. Hasan, much moved by fear of hell, was wont to weep long over his sins. Once when Rabi'a saw him so exercised, she reproached him, saying that his weeping came from pride of self. Rather, she said, weep that through weeping you may open yourself till you find the Lord of Might.

This endorsement of the weeping that leads to knowledge gives a crucial insight into Rabi'a. Despite her words to Hasan and despite the love and joy for which she was celebrated, she was also much given to tears, both of repentance and of rapturous love, and the two were sometimes one.

For these tears were not tears of desperation or self-pity, nor of self-attached wallowing in her own emotions. They were tears of *knowing*, tears that uncork bottled-up feelings or planes of awareness within and so open the way for richer levels of intimacy with God and others. Through intimacy with another, through sharing a broad range of feelings from sorrow to rapture, we *know* the other—and in the process, ourselves—in a way no monochromatic experience, however exalted, could provide. And in knowing is joy.

Thus a key feature of Rabi'a's mysticism was her spiritualization of normal human emotions, both of happiness and distress, rather than seeking to negate them. She spoke of God as friend and lover, rejoicing in his beauty and delight.

Above all, Rabi'a's way with God was a way of *uns*, in the Arabic term: deep intimacy. As we have seen, intimacy

The ways are various, the way to the Truth is but one; and those who travel on the way of truth must go on their road alone.

—'Abd al-Wahid (Sufi mystic)

Sell this present world of yours for the next world, and you shall gain both in entirety.

—Hasan of Basra

I have made Thee
the Companion of
my heart,
But my body is available
for those who seek
its company,
And my body is friendly
towards its guests,
But the Beloved of my
heart is the Guest
of my soul.

—*Rabi'a*

between human beings may be pervaded by joy so strong that neither person can conceive of life without it. Yet over that deep joy may be cast transitory elements of different texture: remorse concerning offenses one thinks one has committed toward the other; yearning and hope for even deeper intimacy and faith that it can come; happiness in moments together that are pleasant, yet not supremely joyous; ecstatic rapture in the heights of union; profound joy in plumbing its depths.

Mystics and lovers alike confide that the relation of two who become one is a complex intimacy compounded of all these aspects. We are not surprised, then, to find that Rabi'a's love for God was characterized by a broad range of nuances. We read of her tears, her transcendent calm, her charity and austerity, her radiance of face. She turned from one to the other like a planet showing different faces to the sun, and all was within the orbit of love. Love and joy are closely related, as we have seen. Love is joy in the world of relationships. It seeks to articulate the joyous unity of being that is already there on a deeper level. But love may move through rainbows of superficial feelings, some other than joy, to express the range of its yearnings.

Rabi'a of Basra, then, was a saint who windowed divine joy into the world through rich love for God as the supreme beloved. The way of love is one path to deep joy. It is one trod by millions at least some length of the way, though doubtless few have followed it as far as the former slave girl who became a shining light of Islam.

A Joyous Ragtag

Yet there are ways other than the transcendent love affair, for joy is joy. Love, joy, and oneness are the three corners of the spiritual universe, and none can exist independent of the other two. But a different emphasis can be gained by realizing the unnamable ultimate, full of joy—call it the Unborn Mind or the Eternal Child—within our prison of self-conditioned reality.

This was the way of Pu Tai, the roly-poly Chinese monk.

His original name is unknown; his monastic name as a monk of the Chan tradition (the school of Buddhism better known by its Japanese title, Zen) was Ch'i T'zu. That is an enigmatic Zen name meaning something like "related to this." It seems to make the statement: "My only name is that I am related to the unnamable Being of the Universe, which is here and now and everywhere." But people called him Pu Tai (in Japanese, Hotei), "cloth bag," because he always carried a big sack around with him, and also because his ample proportions suggested he was something of a food sack himself.

He lived in tenth-century China, and anecdotes about him abound. More than with our other two saints, much of what is reported of Pu Tai is legend and hearsay. But we could not explore the world of spiritual joy and leave out the figure who more graphically than anyone portrays that joy in all its charm and richness.

At the entrance of countless Chinese temples, the worshipper is greeted by an image of an immensely fat,

When I'm hungry I eat; when I'm tired I sleep.

—Zen master Huihai, when asked how he practiced Zen

bare-bellied man with twinkling eyes, a huge grin, and carrying a sack. In homes both Eastern and Western, even more images proliferate, whether of bronze or porcelain, whether objects of worship or curios. Sometimes in these representations as many as eighteen children are crawling over Pu Tai or getting a ride in the bag slung over his back.

Though seldom honored in temples outside China, Pu Tai is popular in Japan and other parts of East Asia. He is a familiar figure in folklore and popular art. He is commonly represented in Japan, for example, on *netsuke*, those small carved toggles for kimono sashes that are favorites of collectors; in this capacity his huge belly, expansive smile, and gaggle of children once accompanied many thousands of people going about their daily business in the island empire. It was as if China, Japan, and the rest of East Asia—a quarter of the world—had decided that a pantheon of the sacred ought to give prominent place to this fat, jolly, wide-smiling, child-loving style of holiness.

Sometimes the raggedy old fellow was even identified with Mi Lo (in Sanskrit, Maitreya; in Japanese, Miroku), the coming Buddha of the future. With a characteristic Chinese concreteness, his huge abdomen tells us that in the paradise on earth he will bring with him, everyone will have enough to eat and more. To Pu Tai himself is attributed a poem that hints at this identity as the exalted secret of his life: "Mi Lo, true Mi Lo / Reborn innumerable times, / Manifested age after age, / Unrecognized every time."

Legend has it that Pu Tai would come around to marketplaces—nobody quite knew from where—and beg everything in sight. He would eat a bite or two of each kind of food he gathered and throw the rest in his huge sack. He slept by the roadside; it is said he could sleep even in the snow without ill effect.

Naturally, his bag interested everyone. Children were fascinated with it and sometimes tried to snatch it from him. Once in a while Pu Tai would open it and spread out its contents so everyone could see, strewing all over the ground the bits of food, straw sandals, bowls, even sticks and stones and assorted rubbish. He would solemnly pick up items one by one, saying, "Look at this!" and "Look at that!" or quizzically asking, "What is that?" and "What is this?"

Indeed, the bag was so full of junk that it suggested all the clutter of an ancient universe, wrapped up and slung over one's shoulder, but still capable of entertaining children. Once, when asked how old he was, Pu Tai responded by saying, "My bag is as old as space." He insinuated that his bag was like the bellows to which the *Tao Te Ching* of Lao Tzu compares the universe: always emptying and giving, yet always refilling and never failing.

When asked a philosophical question, Pu Tai would answer with the "Great Silence" for which Zen masters are famous, and the bag had a part in those responses. Once, when someone put to him the celebrated question, "Why did Bodhidharma (the monk who brought Zen to China) come from the West?" Pu Tai put down his bag and stood there, arms crossed and mouth silent. When the questioner persisted, he picked up the bag again and walked off. He did this again when another monk asked him simply, "What's in your bag?" Pu Tai put it down and stood there

In spring, hundreds of flowers; in autumn, a harvest moon;
In summer, a refreshing breeze; in winter, snow will accompany you.
If useless things do not hang in your mind,
Any season is a good season for you.

—The Gateless Gate
(Zen text)

with crossed arms. "What do you mean by that?" the other insisted. Pu Tai picked up his bag and walked off. On another occasion, when he tried to beg a coin from a monk, that worthy said, "If you show me the Tao (the universal way), I will give it to you." Pu Tai dropped his bag and stood there with crossed arms.

One sign suggests that he was, as his name indicates, related to the nameless Whole. He had a sure sense for predicting the weather. When it was going to rain, he wore wet sandals, and oddly, when it was going to be warm and sunny he wore nails under the soles of his sandals and slept on a bridge. He was always right about the weather, and the farmers, who were his friends, probably appreciated the gift.

More than that, the weather knack can be taken as a sign of two things: first, that he was so deeply attuned to the reality of nature that he intuitively knew what it was about to do; second, that his was not a mysticism of withdrawal from the sensory world but one profoundly aware of it, seeing things accurately just as they are. In this he was very much in the Zen tradition that helped produce the great landscape paintings and nature poetry of China and Japan.

The story is told of an old Chinese Zen master who once said, "Before I studied Zen I saw mountains as mountains and rivers as rivers. When I had made some progress in Zen, I no longer saw mountains as mountains and rivers as rivers. But when I had reached the heart of Zen, I once again saw mountains as mountains and rivers as rivers." That must have been where Pu Tai was.

The universe is another name for infinite consciousness.

—Sokei-an

Three Who Were Joyous

Once when D. T. Suzuki, the modern Zen advocate who did so much to popularize Zen in the West, related that saying in a lecture, a questioner asked him what was the difference between the first seeing of mountains and rivers and the last. Suzuki answered, "No difference, except the second time, from about two feet off the ground." Presumably Pu Tai's immense grin of unbounded deep joy tells us he was at that place also.

Pu Tai was a poet. His poems tell us his way was the way of the white clouds, a way where there is neither sinner nor saint but only the pearl-bright Unborn Mind, where one walks an endless high trail with no destination because one is already Home. Yet out of this realm of trackless freedom comes an immense roar of joy, a sensitivity to the way the wind blows, and an exuberant compassion that made him friends with children and the ordinary folk of the marketplace.

The renowned Zen Oxherding Pictures could have been about Pu Tai, for they show the spiritual seeker ending up where he started. In these pictures, a child sets out to find a lost ox, which represents the true enlightened mind. First he spots its tracks: these represent the traces of enlightenment in scripture and doctrine. Finally he locates the ox, and with considerable struggle manages to bridle and tame it, in the end riding nonchalantly on its back under a full moon. Then the ox disappears, leaving only the child (now a mature man), for when one has found enlightenment it is no longer something separate from oneself. Next, both man and ox vanish and there is only the round whiteness of the universal One—no longer seeking mountains as mountains and rivers as rivers.

Finally, though, the seeker, now a gnarled elder, returns home, which he sees just as he left it. Then, in a common final scene, he becomes Pu Tai. Here we see a jolly, ragged, bare-bellied fellow going down the road into the city "with bliss-bearing hands," stopping on the way to play and laugh with children, for in his true enlightenment he is utterly unselfconscious about time or dignity or anything except his overflowing joy that he wants to get more of by giving it away. The poem and commentary traditionally associated with this picture say:

> Barefooted and naked of breast, I mingle with the people of the world.
> My clothes are ragged and dust-laden, and I am ever blissful.
> I use no magic to extend my life;
> Now, before me, the dead trees become alive.

Comment: Inside my gate, a thousand sages do not know me. The beauty of my garden is invisible. Why should one search for the footprints of the patriarchs? I go to the market place with my wine bottle and return home with my staff. I visit the wine shop and the market, and everyone I look upon becomes enlightened.[10]

Pu Tai had the lightness that goes with great spiritual joy. People who have that joy seem so full of bubbly life that they keep popping up unexpectedly. Even death can't always hold them. There are reports of Pu Tai's entry into Nirvana at the portico of a certain temple—then stories that he was afterward seen puttering around in order to return someone's sandal he had inadvertently carried off to the grave.

For all we know, he and his big grin may still be somewhere, dragging around that huge universe-bag and playing with the children along the way.

A Light-Filled Monk

One day in about 1830, in the old Holy Russia of czars and onion-domed churches, four nuns were walking through a field of high grass with an aged monk who was widely accounted a saint. Father Seraphim, the monk, was walking ahead and talking. Suddenly he stopped and told the nuns to proceed. They did so, but being curious, soon turned back to look at their counselor. To their astonishment, they reported, Seraphim was walking above the grass, lifted up in the air. The nuns fell at his feet, while he urged them, "O my joys (he called everyone he met 'My Joy'!), don't tell anyone about this while I am still alive."[11]

This was the priest and monk St. Seraphim of Sarov. As Rabi'a was a saint of love for God and Pu Tai one of inward realization, Seraphim may be termed a saint of transfiguration. He was so filled with God's light that it illuminated him and shone through him. The light gave him not only radiance but also lucid spiritual wisdom and a deep insight into the needs of souls that came to him. Some say he also had foreknowledge of the suffering and persecution of religion that was to be Russia's lot in the century after his.

There are other accounts of his levitating. Toward the end of his life, fellow monks, coming upon the holy man in prayer, sometimes discovered that his rapture had raised

But I, when I am lifted up from the earth, will draw all men to myself.
—*Jesus, John 12:32*

him up off the floor. Seraphim always requested that they say nothing about it till after his death. He also had a gift of healing which led to many stories of miracles.

According to Scripture, however, the devil is capable of working wonders, but when the miracle seems like sheer overflowing of light and love and divine grace so great that the ordinary working levels of nature cannot contain them, then we can assume that the person involved is one exceptionally close to the pure joy and being that undergirds the world: in common parlance, a saint.

The saint known as Seraphim was born in 1759, in the small city of Kursk in south-central Russia, a city with a bloody past and later the site of a great World War II battle. In Seraphim's day, however, it was quiet and charming. His childhood name was Prokhor Moshnin. He lost his father at an early age and was raised by his mother, a capable woman who continued her husband's housing construction business and was known for her compassion for the poor and for orphans.

At age ten Prokhor became seriously ill. He recounted a vision of the Virgin Mary, who promised to heal him, and he got well a few days later. This experience deepened his natural spirituality. Never really destined for any other vocation, at nineteen, with some friends, he entered the great monastery of Sarov, far to the north and deep in primeval forests. Thus he inaugurated a career as an Orthodox priest and monk that ended only with his death in 1833 at age seventy-three.

The course of his career was not always easy. Seraphim received permission to live in a hermitage in the

When saints become saints, they begin to work.
—Johannes Eckhart

woods, where with youthful zeal he followed a path of great asceticism, which left him weak and often ill, his body covered with sores. But even at this early stage he was becoming filled with exceptional grace, which showed itself in remarkable rapport with animals. He was seen gamboling playfully with a huge bear as though it were a friendly dog. When he went up to the monastery for his rations, the forest animals and birds eagerly waited at his doorstep, and he fed them upon his return.

On the other hand, while in the woods he did titanic battle with the powers of darkness. He heard the voices of demons and even saw their hideous visages; he suffered strong temptation and deep despair before finally overcoming them. If that were not enough, he was attacked and beaten nearly to death by brigands; he had to return to the monastery for a long recuperation.

Going back once more to the hermitage, he entered a period of growth in deep contemplative prayer marked by long periods of enclosure and silence. When he finally emerged, he took up the calling of *staretz*, a position much celebrated in Russian Orthodoxy. The staretz is a person famous for holiness and asceticism who has become spiritual guide and counselor to believers of all backgrounds.

Now, except for occasional periods of retreat, he left the door of his cell open, and so great was his fame that seldom was the man of God without a stream of visitors seeking his advice, healing, blessing, absolution, or simply prayers.

His purification and preparation required so much inward deepening that he was over sixty before this final stage of his life as staretz began. Little more than a decade

And what is a merciful heart? . . . It grows tender and cannot endure hearing or seeing any injury or slight sorrow to anything in creation. Because of this, such a man continually offers tearful prayer even for irrational animals and for the enemies of truth and for all who harm it, that they may be guarded and forgiven.

—St. Isaac the Syrian

was left him. But the arduous struggle toward the transfigured humanity he exemplified at the end was well worth the time, for seldom has a decade of a life spiritually influenced time and place as did Seraphim's. Pilgrims who came to him in search of God's grace ranged from Czar Alexander I to humble soldiers and peasants; Dostoevsky was among the writers deeply affected by him; and when he was finally canonized by the Russian Orthodox Church in 1905, it was in recognition that he exemplified all that was best in its spiritual tradition.

Like Pu Tai, Seraphim had a special love for children and could never resist those who knocked on his door. He could forget his prayers and his older petitioners to play with visiting children as though he were a child himself. For a monk in the Orthodox tradition, he also had a marked openness toward women. Women, whether alone or accompanied, were always welcome in his cell for counsel. He was spiritual father of a nearby community of nuns. He devoted much energy to their affairs, both practical and spiritual and, as we have seen, spent time with them in informal settings—a walk in the fields—as well as in his official capacity.

All this offended the straitlaced, leading to some difficulties with ecclesiastical superiors and to the evil atmosphere created by malicious rumor. His later trials, caused by human jealousy and slander, were sometimes almost as great as his earlier combat with demons. But his manifest holiness carried the day.

This is exemplified in an incident in November 1831, when Nicholas Motovilov, a lay friend of Father Seraphim,

Light, God's eldest daughter.

—*Thomas Fuller*

was talking with him about the power of the Holy Spirit and how to obtain it. The saint's explanation seemed very simple to Motovilov, for Seraphim taught that the Holy Spirit would come to all who prayed and prepared themselves by devout living. The disciple felt there was something he did not yet understand, for although he thought of himself as a serious Christian, he had known the Holy Spirit far less than his mentor.

Finally Father Seraphim told him a deeper secret: we are *already* in the Holy Spirit—now. We have only to realize it. He asked Motovilov to look at him. Astounded, the latter said he could not, for light was shining from the saint's face and eyes, so brilliant that Motovilov was dazzled. But Seraphim told his disciple that he should not be afraid, for he himself was shining just as much. The saint said he had merely prayed for the disciple to have the grace to see clearly. Motovilov described what happened as they thus walked and talked in a snowy valley:

Then I looked at the Staretz and was panic-stricken. Picture, in the sun's orb, in the most dazzling brightness of its noon-day shining, the face of a man who is talking to you. You see his lips moving, the expression in his eyes, you hear his voice, you feel his arms round your shoulders, and yet you see neither his arms nor his body nor his face; you lose all sense of yourself; you can see only the blinding light which spreads everywhere, lighting up the layer of snow covering the glade, and igniting the flakes that are falling on us both like white powder.

"What do you feel?" asked Father Seraphim.
"An amazing well-being!" I replied.

After six days Jesus took with him Peter, James, and John the brother of James, and led them up a high mountain by themselves . . . His face shone like the sun, and his clothes became as white as the light.

—Matthew 17:1, 2

"But what exactly is it?"

"I feel a great calm in my soul, a peace which no words can express."

"And what else do you feel?"

"A strange, unknown delight."

"What more do you feel?"

"An amazing happiness fills my heart."[12]

If but ten among us lead a holy life, we shall kindle a fire which shall light up the entire city.

—St. John Chrysostom

When, by cleansing our own windows of perception or through the prayers of a saint, we encounter the tremendous spiritual reality beneath the visible universe, it turns out to be strange delight and amazing happiness, and it can transfigure us as it did Seraphim and his friend.

Father Seraphim died kneeling in prayer before an icon of the Virgin of Tenderness. When the monks found him, they discovered that nearby on his lectern the pages of the Gospels were mysteriously smoldering.

Three saints of joy. What do they have in common? First, they share an implicit realization that ultimate joy—call it intimacy with God, the Buddha-nature within, the Holy Spirit—is both the ground of our being and something deep within the self; that it is not summoned from far across land and sea, but is already here, close at hand.

Second, this awakening or seeing not only brings deep joy but expresses itself through a sort of holy freedom, spontaneity, openness to all—birds and animals, men and women, and especially children. It is not rigorous or blue-stocking religion but something wider and wiser that rejoices in God because it is sure of God within as love, light, and joy. Third, coming to this place involves trials and a course of spiritual struggle.

We shall now outline the structures of that struggle in a way that can be applied to our own lives.

— *Entering into Joy* —

Thomas Merton said that for him, "To be a saint is to be myself." In which situations do you feel most yourself? In which ones, on the other hand, do you usually feel that "This is just a role I'm playing," or that "I'm deprived of something important." The next time you're in a negative situation, think, "I can truly be myself now, too. If I do this difficult thing well, I'm a saint." Then do it well!

According to ancient alchemy, base metals like lead and iron can be transmuted into gold. List three occasions when you felt strong emotions usually considered negative, such as anger, fear, sorrow, or depression. What have you learned from these occasions—at the time and now? What preceded each event, and where did it lead your inner life? Have you found the gold?

On a short walk, note anything that stirs up feelings of anger, fear, disgust, or sadness—a dead animal, someone quarreling or being reckless, or shabby surroundings. For a moment, just bless the situation. Do your feelings change? Try inwardly sending it peace and joy for the rest of your walk.

Find an image of (or simply visualize) your favorite saint. Look deeply into his or her eyes until you catch a little of that saint's joy—real sanctity is caught, not taught!

Part Three

Discovering Joy
for Ourselves

Chapter Six

How Do We Begin?

SAINTS ARE WONDERFUL, but it may seem that they live on mountain peaks while we are stuck in the valleys. Valleys can be sometimes pleasant and sometimes stifling, but they are always valleys compared to those peaks, whose slopes may appear hopelessly steep.

For one thing, Rabi'a, Pu Tai, and St. Seraphim were celibate and free to embrace lives of holy poverty. Most of us have to find what deep joy we can in the midst of the tensions and hassles of married life, child-rearing, and making a living in a competitive business, professional, or industrial world. Undoubtedly, there are married workaday saints who beautifully exemplify spiritual joy. You may know some yourself. But for various reasons, most of those we know from history have been of the monk or nun variety.

For one thing, monks and nuns have sacrificed much in order to attain and show the world what spiritual heights are possible; they are most likely to go public and be widely recognized for their spiritual joy. For another, the records in such matters are most likely to be kept by members of the ecclesiastical establishment who naturally want to honor their own. We ought, then, to learn what we can from them without feeling that their different lifestyle erects an impossible barrier. They themselves would certainly not want anyone to feel that way, for they gave their lives to sharing their spiritual treasures with all who would receive.

Our fundamental premise is that joy is the basic reality of the universe, that it comprises our innermost nature, and therefore is accessible at all times. Yet, in the world of appearances, some seem to have joy and some not. You meet many people who are glum, angry, burned out, or just going through the motions. Once in a while you meet someone who is bubbling over with joy. As often as not, there is no discernible reason why one is happy and another is not—the joyous person has had rough spots on the road of life; the glum person, opportunities to find happiness. Let's focus on those who seem to have discovered the treasure. You go into some obscure shop, you bump into someone at a big reception or at church or a meeting, and

I walked down and sat on the river's edge, watching the dead wood in its speedy descent to the sea. With neither reason nor provocation, a smile emerged on my face, and finally I saw, and knew I had seen. I knew: the smile itself, that which smiled, and that at which it smiled, were One.

—Bernadette Roberts

you sense it—that person is *really* joyous; that person knows the cosmic secret.

Not that he or she is necessarily giggling or cracking jokes all the time. Humor is a great gift and we need more of it, but it is not the same as joy. What the joyous person has is a radiance, a smiling serenity accented by a twinkle. That person may be of any religion or none, and may or may not have a theological explanation for his or her price-less gift. But whether or not the treasure is named or known, it is apparent. We can only respond with our own joy of appreciation.

Why do some people find it and others do not? Some would say it has to do with karma and past lives; others would credit God's grace according to his sovereign will; still others might adopt the language of psychoanalysis to speak of childhood security and successful individuation. The purpose of this book is not to sort all that out on a theoretical level; rather, it is to help those of us who don't fully experience deep joy and want more of it. As the Buddha put it, a man shot by an arrow doesn't need to know everything about the make of the arrow or why in the world it is there; he needs someone who can extract it. Similarly, we don't need to know everything about why the treasure of joy seems to be out of our immediate line of vision; we need to know how to find it.

A treasure can be obtained in different ways. Sometimes it comes easily by inheritance. Sometimes it appears by dumb luck—a person just runs across it without even looking for it. But for most of us, the surest way is to acquire a map and set out on a deliberate quest. The good news is

Something hidden . . . Something lost behind the Ranges. Lost and waiting for you. Go!

—*Kipling*

Here in a lonely little room I am master of earth and sea, And the planets come to me.

—*Arthur Symons*

that there are such maps to joy—maps drawn by the great saints and mystics for plotting out the high trails of the spirit that lead us back home to being, knowledge, and bliss.

The map we present here follows the classic work *Mysticism*, by the great English Christian authority, Evelyn Underhill. Her examples come mostly from the famous mystics of Western Christendom. But since her outline of the stages of the spiritual life seems congruent with the experience of mystics in all traditions, we can supplement her examples with illustrations from the East as well as the West.

The goal of the aspirant for spiritual wisdom is entrance upon a higher plane of existence; he is to become a new man . . . If he succeeds, his capabilities and faculties will receive a corresponding increase of range and power.

—H. P. Blavatsky

Entering into Joy

1) One student said, "While commuting to work on a tree-lined street each morning, I remind myself that I am in 'heaven' now because I am in the perfect world and do not have to die to experience God—because everything is connected and all is love."

Sometimes an everyday action can lead to insight because its routine nature frees the mind. Perhaps it is gardening, or sitting by a river, or even driving to work. To prepare for constructing your spiritual road map, think about what experiences in your own life might help you shift into a receptive state. You may want to go to your favorite place, close your eyes, and listen quietly for a sense of the Divine.

2) Who in your life radiates joy? It could be someone you know well or someone you just met. What are that person's positive qualities that most attract you? As an exercise, explore in writing the possibility that these same qualities are hidden treasures in yourself, waiting for you to find them. When a problem arises in the future, ask yourself how the joyful person you know would handle it and experiment with acting the same way.

Chapter Seven

A Spiritual Road Map

*E*VELYN UNDERHILL FOUND five basic stages in spiritual development: Awakening, Purification, Illumination, the Dark Night of the Soul, and Union with God. Charting them out provides her road map to the Infinite—a map without borders, which is the best kind.

At the outset, we must emphasize that a map is not the terrain itself. It inevitably oversimplifies and makes schematic what in practical experience may be quite different for different people. Several travelers going between the same two places using the same map may have very

The mystic, therefore,
seeks to pass from what
is finite to what is
infinite . . . and,
in the end,
to become
Being itself.

—*Margaret Smith*

*K*now . . . thou of
the Secret Path, its pure
fresh waters must be used
to sweeter make . . . that
mighty sea of sorrow
formed of the tears
of men.

—*H. P. Blavatsky,*
The Voice of the Silence

different trips. One may take the drive on a sunny day, another in a thunderstorm. One may have a smooth-running new car, another a flat tire or even a complete breakdown or collision. One may stay right on course, another get lost on some side road.

Underhill rightly acknowledges that mystics are a diverse lot. Her summary of the mystical experience will not apply in every case. Some people have become great souls by living only one or two of the steps, but living them very well. Some appear to skip one or two stages entirely, or perhaps experience two or more simultaneously. While many have found a definition of stages (such as the one that follows) helpful in their own spiritual development, it would be disastrous to think of it as a checklist you go through, coming out at the other end a certified saint. Human life, especially an aspect of it as inward and subtle as spirituality, is not that simple. We can and must let each flower bloom in its own time and in its own way.

Nonetheless, road maps are valuable, as are books on botany that describe the normal development of blossom from bud, even though each trip, like each flower, is different. First, the map assures us that there *is* a path and a goal, that the path has been taken before and the goal reached. In our spiritual lives, as in a difficult journey, that knowledge is in itself sometimes deeply comforting. Second, a map gives us something with which to compare our own experiences, whether identical or not, and to gain some idea of what is happening to us. When we are in the pits of a Dark Night of the Soul, for example, it can be helpful to realize that others have also been there and emerged to something far better than they had known before.

You might complain that the following map may be valid for saints and mystics, but you are not one of them, at least in this life. Maybe not, though don't limit yourself in advance. But even those who don't scale the Himalayas can climb smaller hills. If you don't experience the dark night of the soul as profoundly as St. John of the Cross or you aren't transfigured with divine radiance as brilliantly as St. Seraphim, you still have spiritual ups and downs. John and Seraphim can tell you much about how to deepen those experiences and make them more creative.

Let us, then, turn to the way stations along the Infinite Path, according to the route Evelyn Underhill mapped.

Awakening

In order to begin, something must call to your attention the joys of the spiritual life. Sometimes such awakening experiences are intense, fervent, and perhaps unexpected religious inspirations—what may be called conversion or born-again experiences. Sometimes they are calm, rather intellectual decisions to try spiritual development—out of boredom, discontent, or even revulsion at one's present way of life. Sometimes one changes only gradually to deeper spiritual values, and no single moment can be pointed to as the Awakening.

A natural event can serve as a sign. The celebrated Chinese Buddhist monk Mao Tzu-yuan found his thirst for

I see a great mountain standing in space, with a road that winds round . . . until the summit is reached . . . We see how it ends at the summit of the mountain—that leads to a mighty Temple, a Temple as of white marble, radiant, which stands there shining out against the ethereal blue.

—Annie Besant

What appears to be a journey, then, is really an interior movement . . . The paths to be searched for are within us.

— Joy Mills, writing of **The Voice of the Silence**

*J am not sitting;
I am on a journey.*

**—A woman recluse who
lived in one small room**

enlightenment aroused by hearing the call of a crow at midnight. On other occasions, Awakening seems to be stirred by the rhythms of human life. Richard M. Bucke, in his well-known book, *Cosmic Consciousness*, tells us his Awakening came after an evening with two friends reading the poetry of romantics such as Wordsworth, Shelley, and Whitman. As he was riding home, mulling over their ideas in quiet enjoyment, he suddenly felt as though wrapped in flame. A surge of immense joy burst upon him, which he described as "Brahmic splendor." His quest from then on was to understand this state better, and his book is his attempt to compile and interpret the experiences of many mystics.

Some experience Awakening as a supernatural call. Whether we interpret these accounts literally or psychologically, they are an important part of the literature of mysticism. The shamans of indigenous cultures, like many modern-world aspirants to a higher life, believe that they hear the voices of gods or spirits summoning them. So did the prophet Samuel. Early in his career, St. Francis of Assisi heard the painted lips of a crucifix in a broken-down place of worship command him to "repair my church."

Awakening may come through a discovery of the misery and transitoriness of the world as it is. According to tradition, the Buddha was raised as a prince in a sheltered life of luxury and pleasure. While still a young man, he took four chariot rides outside the palace. On each he confronted evidence of the real human world with its suffering and mortality: an aged man, a dying man, a corpse. Then he saw a peaceful holy man with his robe and bowl. This brought home to the young prince the meaninglessness of a life devoted to pleasure in the face of old age, sickness, and death. Inspired by the monk, he realized he could live for no other end but finding and sharing a way to inner joy, despite what is in store for us. This was the beginning; it was six more years until his legendary enlightenment.

Awakening, like the other stages, can be full of unique blessings, but it also has its unique temptations and dangers. No rapture is so intense as that of the beginner to whom the power of the spiritual world has first become unveiled. But for that very reason, the experiencer may be tempted to feel that he or she has now found God in all divine fullness, and that whatever belief system is associated with the experience is the final truth.

Actually, of course, no single experience, however powerful, can reveal more than a tiny portion of the infinite, and only with much seasoning and maturation can even that tiny portion be rightly understood. The awakening experience opens the door a crack, and it is significant beyond words that the door is opened. But this opening is only a beginning.

Awakening experiences can be intense, but they are also likely to be one-sided, more emotional than deeply comprehending, and (as we noted in the first chapter in regard to emotional experiences) likely to be inchoate and to come and go. That may in turn leave the novice mystic on a roller-coaster ride between high elation and deep despair. He or she, finding that the newly-come grace has gone, may wonder whether some terrible sin has come between the soul and God, or if God, for mysterious reasons, has withdrawn his blessing.

The best, the happiest moments of life are these delicious awakenings of the higher powers.

—Emerson

I felt in this moment a profound wound, which was full of delight and of love—a wound so sweet that I desired that it might never heal.

—Madame Guyon

page 73

The essence of purgation is self-simplification.
—*Richard of St. Victor*

At this point the individual will almost inevitably mix up religion and preoccupation with feelings. That is not too harmful at the beginning, for the feelings play a sublime role in wakening the soul to transcendence. But such preoccupation is egocentric from the vantage of the saint's calm selflessness, and it must be overcome. That is the task of the next stage.

Purification

The second stage in spiritual development may be called Purification (or if you prefer, Preparation or the Purgative Way). If you are to move on, the tumult of the Awakening stage must be steadied and stabilized. Otherwise, you are likely either to give up the spiritual life in cynicism and disappointment or continue on an immature level of religion, which is really little more than egocentric emotionalism.

The way to stabilize the new Awakening is to force it into the mold of a disciplined life. That life has two aspects. First, times of prayer and meditation should be regularized into a set pattern. That is, they should generally be practiced at the same time and for the same length of time every day, whether you feel like it or not. This helps you move beyond a spiritual life based on emotional moods and whims. Second, you should try to make your entire way of life consistent with your spiritual practice.

The context for Awakening—prayer, meditation, pilgrimage, or whatever—implies some practice by which the experience may be recalled or recapitulated. The disciplined practice you develop may not be exactly the same as the original one, and perhaps should not be, since now you want something to sustain you over time. The form in which the original Awakening took place may or may not be viable as something for you to do every day.

St. Seraphim's Awakening was perhaps the vision of the Virgin Mary he had as a sick child, but the way he stabilized his spiritual life was through the regular prayer and asceticism of the monastery. That was his time of Purification, of purging away the swings of mood and impulse through the self-denial (excessive as it may have been, at least for anyone but him) of the forest hermitage and the preparation of deeper and calmer meditation.

By disciplined practice in this stage, you are getting your spiritual life under control and integrating it with your everyday life. It becomes something you sustain, not something that just happens. At the same time, you learn that perseverance, even when your spiritual life seems dry, is more important than good feelings and sacred thrills. To persevere is to offer ourselves unstintingly to the deep joy of reality instead of just giving up unless we get satisfaction. Out of offering and perseverance come eventually the heights ascended by the great saints.

The same goes for the way you lead your life the rest of the time. If in prayer or meditation you seek calm, joy, and selflessness, but the balance of your life is self-centered and given to unhappy extremes of anger, fear, or depression, obviously something doesn't mesh. This is a bad situation. The great gulf between the two sides of your life

The mind, when trained, is our truest friend; when left untrained and reckless, it is an enemy that won't leave the premises.
—*Pravrajika Vrajaprana*

makes you a split personality rather than unifying your life as good spiritual practice ought to do.

While the calm of meditation or prayer will in time permeate other areas of your life, influences may also flow the other way and make your prayers really prayers (as many are) of self-indulgence. It is much better to get the two sides together by centering your whole life on your spiritual goals.

The *Yoga Sutras* of Patanjali, a classic yoga text from ancient India, makes this point clearly and programmatically. It speaks of eight "limbs" or stages of yoga practice. They are, in translation, abstention from evil, observance of good, the practice of yoga postures, breath control, withdrawal of the senses from the outer world, concentration, meditation, and attaining joyous equilibrium of mind.

Notice the first two. Specifically, you should abstain from harming others, falsehood, theft, incontinence, and greed; you should observe purity, contentment, mortification, study, and religious devotion. The direction is clear: when you set foot on the spiritual path to deep joy, you must give up all that is untrue to yourself and all that harms others, all that caters to the self-centered appetites and passions, and all forms of excess, while taking on a simple lifestyle, an even-tempered frame of mind, and emphasizing higher things.

The *Yoga Sutras* also stress that the ill effects of negative thoughts, words, and deeds that might be no great sin for an ordinary person will be much greater for one seriously engaged in yoga (or any spiritual path). That is because the higher your aspirations—or sometimes attainments—the greater the inner schism created by departures from them. The farther apart the poles of aspiration and behavior, the greater the chance that the whole system will fly off kilter and degenerate into chaos.

At the same time, the *Yoga Sutras* also say there are rewards for what we give up in pursuit of higher things. Just as the Gospels tell us that those who give up lands and houses for the sake of the Kingdom of God will find them returned a hundredfold, so the *Yoga Sutras* say that those who renounce wealth will find that all jewels flow toward them, and those who adopt harmlessness will see all creatures come to them in peace. Whether these sayings are taken literally or metaphorically, they remind us that to sacrifice for the sake of the spirit is to gain far more than we lose.

These matters involve a whole new orientation to life and will take some time and much perseverance for most people to work out, perhaps many years. That is the work of Purification, Purgation, and Preparation. But even in the process of changing your life, you will begin enjoying the first fruits of the mature spirit.

Illumination

In time, if all goes well, you will begin to find deep satisfaction in the spiritual life. Not only are prayers answered, but the act of praying imparts a rich, subtle joy, or even rapture so great it seems the human form can hardly contain it. Meditation and prayer not only develop peace of mind, but likewise can evoke their own state of inner ecstasy so

He is now so
accustomed to that
Divine Presence that he
receives from it continual
succor upon all occasions.
—Brother Lawrence
(of himself)

rewarding that it becomes a pivot of daily life more important than eating and sleeping.

After Purification has dug regular channels for the
flow of spirit and cut away gross attachments to egotism or
emotional ups and downs, these blessings are no longer
haphazard and unpredictable. With the daily practice of
prayer and meditation, they come regularly and give life a
special glow. As St. Teresa of Avila put it, the seeds planted
at the beginning of the spiritual adventure now burst into
bloom. The purgative stage had been like a hopeful time
of weeding, cultivating, and watering the garden; now you
see return from your labors.

Illumination can take many forms. Indeed, Evelyn
Underhill calls the illuminative stage a way within the Way,
for it has its own little progresses and victories. Some people will emphasize prayer and get to know God intimately
as a person with whom they can converse and share all the
joys and problems of life. Some, like Rabi'a, will feel drawn
to a deep love relationship with God, knowing with the
Divine Beloved all the sweet pleasures and bittersweet
crises of human love and more. Others will be possessed by
a sense of the presence of God everywhere, knowing God in
sky and sea and tree and the faces of friends. For some, the
divine within, the nameless reality in the depth of being,
will be all-important. However it occurs, Illumination will
see these discoveries made and paths toward their fuller
realization explored.

This may well be a time of difficulties with conventional religion. You are venturing into new territory that
may challenge old traditions. But you are not so much of a

backwoodsman as to have no need for trail marks and a handbook on flora and fauna. Doctrines of religion that name the immense mystery you are confronting—call it God, the Holy Spirit, the Buddha-nature—add to your confidence in their reality. Religious worship can take on fresh meaning as a way to reinforce and celebrate what is unfolding within. As the illuminative stage takes hold, many people become happily committed to church or temple.

It may seem, in fact, that the illuminative way is what religion is properly all about. What more could you want than rewarding prayer, supportive beliefs, and satisfaction with your religious institution? Indeed, for most religious or spiritually minded people, this stage may seem adequate; it is all they know and as far as they are able to go. To say this is not a put-down of their lives with God; their ranks include many holy and loving saints. Many may be called to no more.

Yet the *Visudhimagga*, a classic Buddhist text on meditation compiled in the fifth century CE, speaks of a pseudo-nirvana in the middle stages of one's meditation path. In the West, authorities like St. John of the Cross speak of spiritual rewards that precede a new purgation and subsequent closeness to God unimagined by the merely pious.

Subtle spiritual imperfections lurk in the illuminative stage alongside its joys and satisfactions. Temptations remain that can lead to disaster if you do not realize that you are still on the road.

The first danger is to think that you have arrived, that your beliefs and practices are all there are and God himself can lead you no further. However, just because you *have*

Love is the one lesson necessary for the soul to learn . . . If this be mastered, all else will follow.

—*S. C. Hughson*

I make it my only business to persevere in His holy Presence, wherein I keep myself by a simple attention and an absorbing passionate regard to God.

—Brother Lawrence

come a long way, those beliefs and practices are so much intertwined with your self-identity that they can easily become a form of egotism, a way of feeling self-satisfied and, what is worse, grounds for comparing yourself favorably to others who seem not to be blessed with your style of religious life. We need to remember that, while doctrines and forms of worship can certainly point us in the direction of God's greatness, God is infinitely more than what can be obtained in the earthen vessels of word and form.

A second and more subtle danger is that you can become attached to spiritual experiences as pleasures, habitual, like those of the table. Along with this may come a fascination with your spiritual life. It becomes a sort of hobby, an interesting concern; you may be continually taking your religious temperature and looking for signs of progress. In short, there is danger of filling up on prayer and meditation, rather than letting them simply be occasions for self-emptying before the infinite.

Finally, Illumination may retain a separation between religion and the rest of life. To be sure, it strives to overcome the division. Yet so long as you think in terms of times and places of worship, by implication other times and places are not so dedicated; so long as you think of ideas and feelings that are spiritual, other thoughts and moods are implied to be far from God. A division is set, in other words, between devotion and work in the world, between God and the world, implying God is not yet all in all.

In the Purification stage, we have seen it is absolutely necessary to dig straight canals for the Spirit, and these are now in full flood. But there may also come a time when their banks must be made level and the waters become a shoreless sea. Before that wondrous tide, however, the aspirant may brutally and unexpectedly be sent an unprecedented drought. The bubbling streams run dry. The old ways and old joys are no more, and all is dust.

The Dark Night of the Soul

Into this dark night souls begin to enter when God draws them forth from the state of beginners.
—St. John of the Cross

The classic description of this stage is by St. John of the Cross, who first called it "the Dark Night of the Soul," but its darkness has been known to many who have ventured far up the mountain of spiritual experience. The *Visudhimagga* tells us that, after the sunny pseudonirvana stage, there may come a time when its ecstasies fade away and instead the chief experiences are fear and depression. These emotions are induced by a growing apprehension of the emptiness of all conditioned reality, including even the highest spiritual bliss while it is still tainted by any trace of ego. This frightening realization should motivate you to make a strenuous effort to reach the full enlightenment now beckoning from the other side of that slough.

At the time, however, the Dark Night may seem more like a sign of the futility of religion than a call to deeper faith. No doubt many, having gotten this far, have given up under its arid storms and lost faith entirely. For it is a spiritual abyss; God seems hidden or withdrawn. The old good feelings associated with prayer and meditation have fled and in their place is only a sense of dryness and emptiness.

Spiritual persons suffer great trials, by reason not so much of the aridities which they suffer, as of the fear which they have of being lost on the road.

—St. John of the Cross

St. John of the Cross says that the greatest affliction of all in this stage, especially for one who has formerly known the riches of God's grace, is the thought that God has abandoned you, leaving you in the real hell: the sense of being without God. It seems at such times either that the Lord of the Universe is fickle and unreliable or that you have committed some great sin that forced God to turn away his face. Either possibility is grim. You feel chaotic and empty, ready to abandon God and religion as shams. It is as though you had been left on a desert at midnight without a compass.

Still, just as desert night air is clean and chill and the stars, though cold and distant, blaze especially brightly, God is there in the Dark Night, but in a different way than before. Now God is less the prayer answerer or warm lover than a cool presence that bespeaks above all utter purity and infinite immensity, beyond human comprehension. You may feel small and very much alone, as people are apt to in a dark night on the desert, but you can also try opening yourself to the cleansing breezes and exhilarating cosmic vistas.

For that is what the Dark Night is really all about. Just as the Illumination is a second and richer edition of the transports of Awakening, so the Dark Night is like a second and deeper purification stage, intended to remove even the subtlest faults and ego attachments before final realization. Although John of the Cross speaks also of a Dark Night of the Senses, when even the most refined sensual delights are shown to be empty, it is the Dark Night of the Soul that is now most profound and significant. For to the person who has experienced the illuminative stage, spiritual joys are those most likely to be objects of attachment and bound up with ego. We may love God, but in the way the drunkard loves drink. The Dark Night is drying out cold turkey from such an attachment to holy intoxication; it can be just as unpleasant as any detoxification, but it is also just as necessary.

The Dark Night is the hardest stage to go through. But if you accept it for the cleansing and laying of new foundations that it is, if you keep flexible and open to the likelihood you are being called to new patterns of spiritual life; if you hold onto even the bare concepts of divine reality and deep joy, you will make it. One day you will wake up and sense that somehow it is now behind you.

Union

The supreme goal of the spiritual life has been described in many ways: enlightenment, liberation, salvation, union with God. Underhill speaks of it as the unitive stage. All these are attempts to define something ineffable— a sense of a life without boundaries, a life of freedom in and with the universe and its divine ground. One is liberated from all fetters, made wise about the way things really are, united with Reality. Like Rabi'a, one is conjoined with the Supreme Lover; like Pu Tai, one can gambol merrily with the village children unselfconsciously; like St. Seraphim, one is transfigured by the Holy Spirit.

Union is freedom from all fetters, from all conditioned reality, in the Buddhist term, whether bondage of the

[The initiate] has also to experience for a moment the condition called Avichi, that which is without vibration . . . It is said to last only for a moment, but to those who have felt its supreme horror, it seemed an eternity, for at that level time and space do not exist.

—C. W. Leadbeater, on the Fourth Initiation of the Adept, which is compared to the crucifixion of Christ

senses or passions of the mind. In describing Union, spiritual writers over and over again use language that has a kind of openness about it, like unsettled territory. One has gone beyond the realm where maps can be made, and compasses work no better than if the whole country had turned into the magnetic pole.

Zen speaks of enlightenment as "the Gateless Gate"; the Buddha himself said of nirvana that it is neither "this world" nor a "world beyond," and that it has "no moon or sun, no coming nor standing nor going; it is unborn, uncompounded, deathless, and the end of all suffering." In the West, the great Christian mystic Jan van Ruysbroeck (1293–1381) wrote:

If the spirit would see God with God in this Divine Light without means . . . he must have lost himself in a Waylessness and in a Darkness, in which all contemplative men wander in fruition and wherein they never again can find themselves in a creaturely way. In the abyss of this darkness, in which the loving spirit has died to itself, there begins the manifestation of God and eternal life.[13]

Waylessness, darkness, knowing God without means, unborn and deathless reality, neither here nor there . . . What these notions seem to suggest is a state in which one is so deeply united with God that one is abroad in God's own immensity and timeless existence, seeing or grasping God no more than the eye can see itself or a pair of pliers can grasp itself, simply sharing God's own perfect freedom and deep joy.

It is the Zen stage of the second seeing of mountains as mountains and rivers as rivers. It is knowing God so intimately that God is not *known* in any ordinary sense; one has ultimate freedom from any ideas, even ideas about God, which can often be the most enslaving of all.

St. Teresa of Avila, with her usual subtle perceptiveness, distinguishes between the illuminative and unitive stages. She writes of that Union with God in which the soul is aware of union and "rejoicing in its captivity." She then describes an even higher state in which "there is no sense of anything but enjoyment, without any knowledge of what is being enjoyed," and yet the soul now "enjoys incomparably more" in contemplative prayer, without any words or ideas coming between the mystic and complete Union.

Another great mystical writer, Meister Eckhart, put it in his pungently paradoxical way when he preached that we must "pray that we may be rid of God, and taking the truth, break into eternity," where we exist in simple desireless being as in the womb, knowing God truly by being rid of the name of God.

Alone yet not alone, just as the fetus in the womb is both alone and symbiotically attached to the mother. In this manner, the unitive mystic, a happy infant in the womb of the universe, is linked by love to all around.

Unitive freedom is not selfish freedom but freedom to love all beings freely. The mystic in the wayless darkness is not an aimless wanderer but follows another kind of compass—love. Ruysbroeck tells us that the mystic lost on those trackless heights must "inwardly cleave to God, with adhering intention and love, even as a burning and glowing fire which can never be quenched."

Buddhism emphasizes that the wisdom of enlightenment must always be joined with compassion, for if wisdom is seeing the interrelatedness of all beings, love is the ethical expression of the same truth: loveless enlightenment is not enlightenment at all but spiritual self-deception.

Indeed, we find that persons who have achieved Union are not only the most joyous people on the earth, but those who are most effective in working for its welfare. These saints are not held back, like so many of us, by mixed motives, nor are they held back by time-consuming piety, as they might have been at an earlier stage. St. Catherine of Sienna spent three preparatory years in a cell praying and practicing great austerities. Then she had an experience of a mystical marriage, which apparently was a breakthrough to Union. She left her cell, greeted her family again, and embarked on an active career that included dealing with popes and sovereigns in her efforts to promote peace.

Such people have arrived where we would like to be. But in a profounder sense we are already there. All the divinity, all the love, all the deep joy in the universe are already in us and all around us. All we need to do is awaken to them, prepare for them, clean out the channels through which they can flow into consciousness.

We will next look at two very effective ways to do this.

What is more ordinary, more of this world, than to feed the hungry, and yet it rates the Kingdom of Heaven.

—*St. Augustine*

A Spiritual Road Map

Entering into Joy

Here are simple ways to enhance awareness at each stage of spiritual growth. You might choose the one you feel describes your present experience, or you might try them all.

Awakening: *Sit quietly in a place that draws you. See if you can feel the oneness between you and the tree, the rock, the wind, the bee, the person sitting next to you. Here is one college student's experience:*

Two friends and I were traveling through Utah when we stopped at a rest point. The setting sun was casting red and purple hues on the tall, powerful, smooth canyon walls. A storm flamed on the horizon—dark clouds and thunder, lightning belching from the sky. It was beautiful. We climbed down into the canyon just because we felt like immersing ourselves further. While nature made its chaos in the distance, we stood shouting into the canyon and listening to the booming echoes. Soon, though, I was just silent. Sometimes, with all the evil in the world, you begin to doubt the existence of a higher being. But standing in that canyon, overwhelmed at the beauty before me, I was sure that God had created it.

Purification: *The purgative stage can range from a program such as Alcoholics Anonymous to a discipline of yoga, prayer, or meditation. But it should be governed by two principles: it must be intentional, and it must be done on a regular, daily schedule—whether you feel like it not. It should not be too ambitious or complex; the important thing is to maintain it over a long term. Choose such a program for yourself. Then*

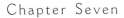

decide if you are really going to do it. How seriously do you want to change?

Illumination: *Think about when you feel most connected to the Divine. If you are affiliated with a church or temple, take a fresh look at your relationship to it. Does it nurture this sense of connection? Is any other path drawing you? One student tells this story:*

I was in the church choir. We were singing a song I did not particularly like. About a minute into it, I remember looking at the mosaic image of Jesus' face on the wall. I don't know why, but I kept staring at it for a long time. Then suddenly I saw His eyes staring back at me. I wasn't even scared. Instead, I felt a very comfortable warmth in my body. It's as if He had been staring at me for a long time.

The Dark Night of the Soul: *Theosophist Charles W. Leadbeater could be talking about this stage in describing what he calls the Fourth Initiation:*

. . . the man shall be left alone entirely . . . all his friends turn against him through some misunderstanding. It all comes right afterwards, but for the time the man is left with the feeling that all the world is against him.

What is the most desolate experience you have ever had? What has it taught you about your strengths and weaknesses? How has it shifted your priorities? How have you moved beyond it?

Union: *This highest mystical stage is paradoxically the most ordinary, in that it can take place while doing the most* *simple things of everyday life—such as one father describes he feels in "hugging my son goodnight and just being aware of our unconditional love."*

For fifteen minutes, practice this meditation as you go about working, driving, caring for children, emptying the garbage . . . Try focusing on the task at hand and yet remaining unbounded in mind so that you sense God and the universe in the present moment. You might pretend you are an athlete performing "in the zone," when action just flows without deliberate thought.

Part Four

Living in Joy
Every Day

Chapter Eight

Opening the Inner Doors

How do we ease our way along to ultimate Union? Various images can help explain the process. Many spiritual writers speak of a path, calling to mind journeying and a high country beyond the ranges. But we can also think of deep joy as something already there: the *ananda* level, in the Vedanta term, of the self. It is present in the depths, waiting to be tapped. It is like water behind the sluice gates of a dam, or like sweet perfumed air trapped behind a closed cobwebbed door. We need to get the door open.

Lift up your heads,
O you gates;
Be you lifted up, you ever-
lasting doors,
that the King of glory may
come in!
—*Psalm 24*

Humor is a prelude to
faith and
Laughter is the beginning
of prayer.
—*Reinhold Niebuhr*

Openness implies movement, communication, unimpeded sight, and free passage. When a door is open, people, vision, words, ideas, feelings can pass freely between two places where they could not before. In a deeper sense, the two places, like two rooms, become part of one system.

So would we have it between our ordinary everyday minds and our true self imbued with the joy of God. There are ways to open the inner door to that other room. In this chapter we will focus on two such ways, both associated with traditional religious practice. We will look at them especially as means to tap infinite joy. These are the ways of meditation and prayer.

Some people will be drawn particularly to one of these and some to the other. However, they are not intrinsically opposed to one another, except in terms of some philosophical/theological definitions. Some people, able to reconcile the conceptual differences, have successfully practiced both. For God is always larger than any concept we can possibly have. No matter what our concept, there is undoubtedly a sense in which other, even seemingly contradictory concepts, are also true.

The main difference between prayer and meditation is that prayer can imply a concept of God as a person other than oneself, whom one addresses as another; whereas meditation can imply that God is a presence deep within. A key to discovering which view you should emphasize lies in what concept of God is most real to you. Do you think of God as the divine other with whom you can have a relationship of conversational intimacy and love? Or is God something immanent that you can realize within yourself?

Opening the Inner Doors

The first may lead to a way of joyous loving prayer, the second to a way of joy-infused meditation. No one way is right for all people, and as we have observed, some seem to find deep joy almost by accident, with no special technique. Others find it through faith, chanting, dance, and many other means.

Suppose you feel drawn by prayer to a personal God rather than by meditation. From the perspective of deep joy, prayer and meditation are not as different as you might suppose.

In meditation, the object is to bring the mind to a settled, still place. People who have wrestled with prayer and know its varieties understand that the prayer we probably begin with—praying for others and for our own needs, or simply for God's will to be done—may lead naturally on its own into prayer of adoration. This is simple, joyous wonder at being in God's presence and awe before his greatness and love. Prayer focused on God frees the mind from its usual rush of activity and brings about the stillness in which joy can arise. In turn, adoration can fuse into a prayer of quiet or of listening, wherein all mortal flesh is silent before God, content simply to enjoy his sweetness or listen to what he may have to say to us in response.

Subtle yet important differences, however, also separate meditation and prayer. There is the joy of uncovering new and rich layers of yourself and the joy of happy interchange with another you love. For prayer is directing love outward, focusing it all on what is envisioned as another—close, perhaps nearer than breathing, yet not identical with yourself as you know yourself, and possessing a mind and

*More things are wrought by prayer
Than this world dreams of.*

—Tennyson

Not by penance, nor by austerities, nor by study is [God] attained; but those who love him with whole-souled devotion find him easily.

—Srimad Bhagavatam

will separate from yours. It is precisely in this exploration of God as another to be increasingly known and loved that joy builds. As the saint Rabi'a knew, prayer is a love affair with God. It can have all the anguish, guilt, and heartaches of any love affair, yet the joy and wonder, the passionate anticipation and delight, far exceed its agonies.

The Royal Road of Meditation

Meditation is the royal road to spiritually-based deep joy. It may not be for everyone, but I am convinced that many could find what they seek through meditation if they knew more about it.

Meditation is really very simple. While, like anything worthwhile, it makes some proper demands on your style of life, it requires no harsh discipline, elaborate mastery of technique, or difficult intellectual assent. It simply allows the mind to take time off to relax and just be itself. This brings inner release, not (as some think) tightening up and concentrating narrowly. It allows mental activity to become still, just as one might allow a bucket of roiled-up muddy water to sit still until the agitation dies out and the mud sinks to the bottom, leaving the water clear.

Most of our mental activity is really reactive. When we're awake—and even often when we're asleep—it seems we always have to think about something. Our thoughts are usually in reaction to some outside stimulus. We see something or hear something and have to respond on some level. Our thinking can also be a reaction to some equally potent

Prayer is as natural to us as speaking, sighing, or gazing, as natural as the beating of a lover's heart.
—*Ernesto Cardenal*

Where there is peace and meditation, there is neither anxiety nor doubt.
—*St. Francis of Assisi*

internal signal. We're hungry or tired or in pain and can't really do anything else until we take care of that need. Or, in the absence of any such immediate jab to react to, the mind—abhorring a vacuum—will dig up something to chew on from the past or future: a worry, hurt, anxiety, or fantasy. Anything to avoid just being itself here and now in the present, unconditioned.

Reactive thinking is not all bad, of course. We have to deal with situations that come our way, and we have to solve our problems by thinking them through. That's what the mind is for. Only that part of mental activity—maybe half of it—that is based on irrational anxieties and pointless fantasies is useless. The purpose of meditation is to stop this activity of the "monkey mind," as it is called in Zen. It is not about problem solving or producing beautiful thoughts. In meditation, the mind simply relaxes and takes time off.

The basic way to stop the monkey mind is through what is called one-pointed meditation. This means bringing the attention to rest on some object. Eventually you will be able to withdraw attention even from that point, and true cessation of active thought will ensue. You will be caught up in deep stillness and peace.

To meditate effectively—and to get near the goal of deep joy—you have to gear your mind down to a much lower ratio than that to which it is ordinarily accustomed. In meditation as in regular life, before you can take a relaxing vacation, you have to learn how to relax—something not everyone can do. There are those who put in as tense a day vacationing in the country as doing business in the city.

When the mind, thus purged by ceaseless meditation, is merged in Brahman . . .[i]n that state there is no sense of duality. The undivided joy of Brahman is experienced.

—*Shankara*

Joy has no name. Its very being is lost in the great tide of selfless delight—creation's response to the infinite loving of God.

—*Evelyn Underhill*

It doesn't matter too much what point of focus you choose. In many respects it is best if it is something low-key and emotionally or intellectually unexciting, so that you don't become reactive to *it!* Many meditation teachers have their students start by focusing on the breath. However, if focusing on something of religious significance would enhance the overall meaning of meditation for you, that is certainly all right. Some people prefer a visual focus—a candle flame, a painted dot, a glint of sunlight, a flower, anything that provides a calming and steady focus of awareness. A religious symbol—a cross or star—can also be used.

The focus can also be auditory. Chanting a mantra or using words like "One . . . one . . . one . . ." or "Joy . . . joy . . . joy . . ." or Jesus' model prayer (also known as the Our Father or Lord's Prayer) are also appropriate. Other possibilities are to focus on a yogic posture or internal visualization, though these are more suitable for those working in the context of the spiritual tradition that employs them.

The point is not to think about whatever you choose as a focus, much less to analyze it intellectually, but just to let the mind rest on it until mental activity stills and you pass into deep quiet and, eventually, deep joy.[14]

The great wonderful secret of meditation is that when the mind is truly still and really itself—fully, without any holdbacks—it is identical with the deep joy at the heart of the universe. Meditation stills all that is not God and joy in the mind, so that the God-joy leaps through unimpeded. In the stillness of meditation this deep joy wells up and up till it seems you can contain no more.

In this light my spirit suddenly saw through all, and in all created things, even in herbs and grass, I knew God, who He is, how He is, and what His Will is.

—Jacob Boehme,
after observing sunlight reflected on a polished pewter dish

The Path of Loving Prayer

The intricacies of the path of loving prayer have been well expounded by the sages of *bhakti*, or devotionalism, in India. The wise Narada, for example, described eleven forms of devotion. They are love for the greatness of God, for his beauty, for his honor, and for recollection of him; there is love for God like that of a faithful servant for his master, of a friend for a friend, of a parent for a child, of a loving husband or wife for a spouse; there is the love expressed in self-consecration to God, in absorption in God, and the love in the pang of separation from God. These diverse loves, which clearly coincide with all the diversity of human love, are benchmarks in the approach of the human soul to the ultimate.

It is likely that you will first simply respond, awestruck, to the greatness of God, gradually coming to love worshiping him and every thought of him. Then you will want to serve God continually, doing his work in the world. But as the worship and service of God bring you into closer intimacy with him, you find yourself knowing and loving God more familiarly. You learn that God encourages his lovers to think of him as friend, as parent or child, as beloved consort with whom you share the deepest and most personal delights.

Yet that is not all. As you devote yourself wholly to God, you may rise (as we have seen) to rich unitive experiences in which there is no whisper of thought of anything but God. By the same token, since this is a way of prayer that pre-

One might be in the thick of the world and yet maintain perfect serenity of mind.

—Ramana Maharshi

The devotee becomes God-intoxicated . . .

—Jadunath Sinha
(following the sage Narada)

Our Father,
Who art in heaven,
Hallowed be thy Name.
Thy Kingdom come,
Thy will be done,
On earth,
As it is in heaven.
Give us this day our
daily bread,
And forgive us our
trespasses,
As we forgive those who
trespass against us.
And lead us not into
temptation,
But deliver us from evil.
For thine is the Kingdom,
and the Power,
and the Glory,
Forever and ever. Amen.

—The Lord's Prayer

supposes God as the beloved other, you are also aware of separateness. The intimacy makes the poignancy, the sweet yearning distress, all the more consuming, but it is a poignancy that now you could not live without. It is a poignancy as sharp as and finally one with joy, a realization of the supreme human condition—that we are creatures who simultaneously live in God and want God. Of this realization, love is the sublime teacher, because love follows the way of deep prayer.

Spiritual authorities tell us that often at the beginning— the Awakening stage—God blesses a soul with a great ecstatic experience as a sort of encouragement or foretaste. He then seems to withdraw during the Purification stage, as if to test the aspirant's discipline, only to return with successively deeper and more stable levels of divine grace in the Illumination and Union stages. If we do not allow God to lead us through the dusty valleys of Purification and later, the Dark Night of the Soul, by maintaining a steady practice, we will miss the greatest joys of intimate life with him.

Prayer, then, first requires method. Just as in a free and spontaneous human love affair, where one sets regular dates for seeing the beloved, so must your love affair with God embrace times and places for prayer. Set a regular time for prayer at an hour when you will be refreshed and at your best—for prayer deserves your best and ought to be zestful—and when you can be reasonably free of interruption. Find a place with the right atmosphere and, if you wish, set it apart in an appropriate way. You can do this by using it only for prayer and placing such objects as candles, incense, and symbols or pictures there.

Opening the Inner Doors

The ways of prayer vary with religious traditions. However, the kind of prayer that leads to joyous intimacy with the divine should be thought of as a conversation with God—though one which, like any lover's conversation, may lead to a closeness beyond words. In intimate conversation, the keynotes are honesty, openness, and the conveyance of love through what you say and the way you say it. The same should characterize prayer. Thus, you do not conceal heartfelt worries, problems, and desires, but try to bring them all into the ambit of love. Nothing is more supremely civilized than good conversation, whether with family or friends or with God.

A good prayer of conversational intimacy may well consist of five parts: invocation, confession, petition, intercession, and adoration. (These can also stand alone as five different kinds of prayer.) *Invocation* is the opening, calling upon God's name. You can linger on it a little, thinking and talking of yourself as in the presence of the ultimate.

Next, since your prayer is to be one of perfect honesty and openness, you should talk about those things that you know have separated or are separating you from God or from the perfect life of the universe. This is known in various religious traditions as *confession of sin* or the Sacrament of Penance. Do more than just enumerate the deeds and attitudes that pull you toward self-centered but transitory goals and away from the sources of deep joy. Take time and leave spaces to receive counsel on each problem.

Next move on to *petition*, which means praying for yourself and your needs or desires. In the prayer of loving intimacy, petition has a place. Some feel it is unworthy, even

May my prayer be set before you like incense: may the lifting up of my hands be like the evening sacrifice.
—Psalm 141:2

infantile, to bring such matters before the throne of the ultimate. Certainly a person who would pray for nothing but a late-model car or even healing from sickness for himself alone would be, to say the least, spiritually undeveloped.

If we know ourselves at all, however, there are things we want, changes we should undergo, places in mind and body that cry out for healing. If our prayer is really to be honest and open, we cannot deny these needs out of some false sanctimoniousness. Just as you sometimes talk about yourself, your desires and dreams, in conversation with close friends, you should also talk about such things in prayerful conversation with God. There is nothing wrong in referring to your wants and needs or concentrating on those things that will help you better serve others. Nevertheless, the final focus should be not on yourself but on opening yourself to God and what God can do in your life.

Now turn your conversation to others in the form of prayer known as *intercession*, which means prayer for others. With love in your heart, lay before God the suffering of the world and needs and well-being of those you know and love. Express your special concerns for peace, for the sick, for the poor, for those who work long and arduous hours, for parents, mates, children, for all you want, in the fine Quaker phrase, to "hold in the light." Think lovingly of each to whom you direct your intention to help. Talk with God about it, for God shares the love you have for all those for whom you pray.

These articulations should indeed open deep planes of consciousness, and in so doing swing wide the doors of love and deep joy. Inner barriers break down as you express

*I say that we are wound
With mercy round and
round
As if with air.*
—Gerard Manley Hopkins

what is closest to you in the face of ultimate reality. As prayer proceeds through confession, petition, and intercession, you may find love and joy beyond measure.

It will be natural, then, to move into the next stage of prayer, *adoration*, when all thoughts of sin or want fall away and you are content just to praise and love God. First this may be in words, like those of the hymns and chants and psalms of all faiths, but finally adoration will move beyond words altogether. Then prayer may unselfconsciously become something very similar to meditation with all its openings to deep joy.

— Entering into Joy —

1) Meditation can bring deep calm. The key is to stop the activity of the monkey mind, as the Zen school calls it, and allow the mind a little quiet time just to be itself as pure consciousness. The way to do this is to focus on just one thing. If you have not meditated before, here are some guidelines.

Find a quiet, uncluttered place where you are not likely to be disturbed. For your first meditation, twelve to fifteen minutes should be about the right time.

Sit cross-legged on a floor cushion or upright in a fairly hard chair. Keep an erect but not rigid posture. Fold or rest the hands gently, close the eyes or focus them softly on a single point.

One focus can be the breath. Simply count your breaths from one to ten; then start over. When your mind wanders—

and it will!—gently return your attention to the breath and begin counting again from one. Other points of focus can be visual (a candle flame, a religious icon) or auditory (repetition of a word or phrase, or listening to a natural sound like falling rain).

Keep up the practice until the mind is very still, then hold the stillness as long as possible without thinking about anything. Then gently bring yourself out of the meditation state. Think about what you have learned from this experience of another state of consciousness.

2) Prayer can mean struggle, tears, even argument with God. But even confessional prayer can also lead to joy. A student wrote:

I think I was about twelve years old. We have a winter prayer meeting at our church. We were praying out loud, confessing our sins and asking the Holy Spirit to be with us. I felt God's hand touching me, and I burst out crying with joyfulness. I still cannot forget that moment.

Recall your deepest moments of prayer, including the times when you confessed and repented your sins. What are your most serious ongoing sins today? Pray about them at length in whatever way seems best, then open yourself to joy and see what happens.

3) Some spiritual experiences transcend categorization as meditation or prayer and are simply a direct connection with the sacred. Such experiences are often associated with music and art. One student reports:

I was watching a musical play. A church choir began to sing a song full of praise and intense spiritual feeling. The lead singer held a note that just seemed to resound throughout the theater. I felt as though it struck a place in my heart. I suddenly began to feel a warm glow deep within myself as a tear came to my eye. For I was thankful for the Lord's many blessings. It was as if he had touched me through a messenger (the singer) and through song.

Listen to the music best able to reach you spiritually. What can you say about the kind of experience it arouses?

Chapter Nine

Creating a Lifestyle for Joy

After prayer, there is the rest of life. So let us return now to another theme alluded to in our earlier discussion of Purification: living a lifestyle in accordance with meditation and spiritual training.

I am convinced that one can get in touch with deep joy in all possible circumstances of human life—as a king on a throne or in the dregs of poverty, in the ordinary comfort of the modern way of life or as an inmate of a concentration camp. Corrie ten Boom, who, with her sister Betsie, was incarcerated in a Nazi camp because they harbored Jews in their native Holland, affirms that Betsie, through her religious faith, radiated peace even amid the horrors of Ravensbruck.[15]

But there are important distinctions to be made here. It is one thing to maintain joy amid hardships or persecutions imposed from outside, either through the vicissitudes of fate or because of the evil of the world. Throughout history, martyrs have discovered that the spiritual calling sometimes brings prison or even death, yet have found amid these very torments the strength to rejoice.

However, it is something else to bring poverty or suffering upon yourself or to live in chaos because you are unable to control your time, rein in your desires, or accomplish your purposes. If you haven't found the power to take charge of your own life, it will be divided, going one way and then another, in a manner incompatible with good meditation or prayer or deep joy.

I emphasize that this is something you can judge only for yourself. To say that a family or a nation is poor because it deserves to be poor or that someone is ill in mind or body because of some sin is a terrible and callous judgment. Who of us knows enough to be absolutely sure of what anyone does or does not deserve? Most of us do not even know ourselves that well. Can we be completely sure that, judged by the same standards we would apply to the rest of the world, we fully deserve what good things have come our way?

In the Purification stage we need to learn to control our own lives. Here you can and must apply strict standards. This stage is all about candid self-examination, purging your

The knower of the Atman does not identify himself with his body. He rests within it, as if within a carriage. If people provide him with comforts and luxuries, he enjoys them and plays with them like a child.
—*Shankara*

life of everything that is inconsistent with your spiritual goals, and setting your house in order.

It is said—and my own experience bears this out—that you can break a bad habit or establish a good habit by carefully not doing the former and doing the latter for one month. Try it: do not overeat, drink, smoke, or whatever the compulsion is, for a month. Then do what you set yourself to do for a month—meditation, regular exercise, good eating, whatever. See if the negative dependency has not lost its power and the good become well established. This is what the purgative stage should mean in everyday terms.

The objective here, as in so much regarding the inner life, is to be decisive with yourself without obsessive fanaticism: this is why the one-month plan is a good idea. Older spiritual writers talk about two dangers to be avoided: rigorism and scrupulosity. *Rigorism* means setting and enforcing for yourself a rule of life that is unnecessarily harsh and unbending; *scrupulosity* refers to excessive preoccupation with and remorse over relatively minor infractions of what you consider to be spiritual obligations. There is great wisdom in these condemnations. The whole point of a spiritual way of life is to facilitate the inner freedom and deep joy of the saints, not to add burdens or give yourself more to worry about. Yet the experience of centuries shows that regularity and discipline are necessary to achieve those goals.

This practice involves finding the point of wise moderation, the exact point of equilibrium between harmful self-indulgence and scrupulosity. It is a subtle matter and may not be exactly the same for every temperament. You need

Here are your waters and your watering place. Drink and be whole again beyond confusion.
—Robert Frost

Only the brave know how to forgive.
—Laurence Sterne

to demand something of yourself without lapsing into an orgy of self-recrimination if you neglect to meditate one day or go to a party and eat or drink too much. You need to be like a supple young tree that, even if bent to the ground, springs back again full of life, not like rigid dead wood that cracks under pressure. Setting up a pattern of daily prayer or meditation requires good common sense.

So far as the rest of your life is concerned, the key is to live in a manner that is congruent with your spiritual practice. Just as these practices are supposed to induce calm joy and a relationship with higher reality, so your lifestyle and surroundings should be calming, tend toward joy, and foster a sense of living for more than sensual and material gratification. Above all, everything should support the deep unity of life. Work and leisure, friendships and family relations, spiritual and secular activities ought not be split off from each other with different values operative in each; rather, they should blend together as much as possible. In the New Testament phrase, let your eye be single. Let your whole life, then, be shaped by the equilibrium, the wise moderation of which we have spoken, neither self-indulgent nor rigorist.

In practice, if you want to find and keep joy, it helps to live in reasonable simplicity, neither in abject poverty nor choked with material goods. Can the goods a consumer society constantly dangles before our eyes bring as much real joy as a single flower or one good book from the library? If you move toward simplicity—living in a clean and neat but unostentatious home, earning an honest living and spending within your means, eating wholesome food and

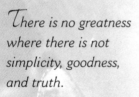

There is no greatness where there is not simplicity, goodness, and truth.

—*Leo Tolstoy*

keeping regular hours, you will set the physical conditions for joy.

However, living moderately and simply does not mean stifling creativity. That would be a disastrous misconception, for apart from love no human activity is closer to the wellsprings of deep joy than creativity. Cultivate it in your own way. If you enjoy cooking, prepare your wholesome food as creatively as possible. Ornament your house with art or furnishings made by yourself or your friends. Spend part of your free time writing or painting. It doesn't matter so much what you do, but find something creative that you like and feel good at, and spend time with it.

It is important to have a collection of books—and, if you wish, tapes and videos—on topics consonant with your spiritual quest, the sort you return to time and time again for inspiration. Related pictures and symbols might be on the walls.

Many people like to read briefly from mystical or religious writings in preparation for prayer or meditation and to focus attention on suitable pictures or symbols. Soothing or inspiring music is also helpful. The means for all this should be at hand, unostentatiously.

Finally, remember that you must not try to push anyone else in the household—spouse or children—into a lifestyle they have not freely chosen. If they choose to live less simply than you or around different values, you must accept this cheerfully and not let it become a source of contention, just as they must accept your way. All this is part of the love and wise moderation of the path to joy. People are not all ready for the same kind of growth at the

*There is no Frigate like
  a Book
To take us Lands away
Nor any Coursers like
  a Page
Of prancing Poetry.*
            —Emily Dickenson

same time, and you can't force the conditions you need on them, any more than you can push the flow of a river. But if you really radiate deep joy, sooner or later they will want what you have.

You can adhere to your meditation or prayer pattern while getting your life in order. But what about the trials that come in anyone's life—hardship, illness, heavy problems? Can you really stay with deep joy in the midst of them? This we shall next consider.

Entering into Joy

Alan Watts's autobiography describes the environment of an unforgettable woman:

I have invented the word "goeswith" to mean the inseparable relationship between different aspects of the same thing.... Elsa invariably goeswith a garden. She learned ... that flowers and vegetables, trees and mountains, animals and birds, are people and must be treated as such....

Shortly after I met her, Elsa moved from Fairfax to a knoll in the Tamalpais foothills.... [She and an architect friend] transformed this area into a paradise, a Garden of Eden, so that a dry land of clay, scrub oak, sage brush, and eucalyptus became a haunt for hummingbirds.

She made a central patio of sundecks sliding into a courtyard surrounded with flowers and cactus plants and a lemon tree and many kinds of fuchsias and strange little lantern-flowers with pointed caps like Tibetan lamas....

Creating a Lifestyle for Joy

Write up a sketch of the ideal home or lifestyle that would best go with your particular spirituality. If you cannot live it at present, keep it in your heart as your private alternative reality and insert it into your life as best you can.

Chapter Ten

For Richer for Poorer, in Sickness and in Health

BAD THINGS DO HAPPEN TO GOOD PEOPLE. The children of loving parents sicken and die, fire and flood strike the just and unjust, war and plague have not yet been banished from the earth. Do these harsh realities make a mockery of deep joy as the fundamental reality, if not ultimately, at least in the commonplace reality of our own lives?

Most of us are not yet saints, invulnerable to whatever life brings—if indeed even saints are that hard-cased or should be. For we, whether saints or not, are human beings, not stones. Any saint, any knower of deep joy, ought to be more fully human, in the best sense, than others. Like Jesus, she or he ought to be able to pipe for those who dance and for those who weep and still not lose hold of a joy that is deeper than tears, joy that is the still point at the center of the dance.

The portrait the Gospels paint of Jesus is of a man who manifested all the rich panorama of human emotions to their purest and fullest. He wept for the dead Lazarus as he also wept in Gethsemane at the hard fate before him. He showed healing compassion above all toward women, children, and the sick. His agony under the lash and upon the cross was in full public view.

But what of his joy? We have hints of it when he graced the wedding feast at Cana, when straitlaced opponents who did not understand the exuberant freedom of the truly holy called him a winebibber and friend of disreputable publicans and sinners. We find it suggested in the wonderful attraction he had for people and in the glory of his transfiguration and resurrection.

But if Jesus had a special relation to the God of the Book of Job, the God who could recall when the morning stars sang together and the sons of God shouted for joy, even these glimpses of joy seem pale compared to what one might expect of Jesus. Could it be that the fullness of his joy was more than this world could now bear? G. K. Chesterton, at the end of his remarkable little book, *Orthodoxy*, suggests just this possibility. Though Jesus displayed all his other feelings unreservedly to the world, when he prayed he arose before dawn and went alone into the mountains. The exchange of a cosmic joy beyond human

The deified soul is . . . authentic, whole, natural, spontaneous, fearless, and strongly itself in every event and situation. God has not fashioned a wimp, weasel, or robot.

—Bernadette Roberts

capacity—an exchange between himself and the reality behind the infinite universe—called him into solitude. He went up, Chesterton says, to conceal his mirth.

Of course, we do not know what really transpired. But the idea of a joy so great as to counterweight Jesus' sorrows and suffering is attractive. Even the notion of these sessions of joy deep in the mountains, amidst a full, varied, totally engaged and *lived* human life, can help us find deep joy in our own varied lives.

How? Here are some suggestions.

Making Time for Joy

Take specific time out to cultivate deep joy. Just as Jesus arose before dawn to go into the mountains to pray, no matter how harried or dangerous the circumstances of his busy life, so we must *make time* to find deep joy no matter what. In times of great suffering, poverty, sorrow, or anxiety—above all, of sadness—it is even more important. No troubled waters are so deep that they cannot be spanned by a bridge. No obligations imposed by troubles are so great that they preclude all recourse to deep joy, even if for only a few minutes saved for prayer or meditation.

Whether before dawn, at noon, or in the evening, set aside time for prayer or meditation. Plug into the joy that is already there. Let it make the rest of your hassled life relax and perk up. I am not talking now about a general attitude, but about a specific time to do nothing but find deep joy—not to worry over anxieties or sort out problems, not even

And so do not neglect this contemplative work . . . When it is genuine it is simply a spontaneous desire springing suddenly toward God like sparks from fire.
—The Cloud of Unknowing

Now was I come up in spirit, through the flaming sword, into the paradise of God.
—George Fox

to do routine prayers, just time to get in touch inwardly, the best way you know, with deep joy—FULL TIME!

The problem is making yourself do it. Troubles have a way of devouring your whole life and are jealous of even a little time devoted to anything else, especially to activities that cut into their monopoly of your mind. When you focus on worry or sorrow, the temptation is to wallow in it, to think you don't have the time or strength for anything else. You say, "I'm just too harried today to meditate. Besides, with all this on my mind, it wouldn't do any good anyway. I'll just skip it."

To make yourself change pace and meditate or pray in those times takes effort. Changing mental gears is painful. It's like getting into a cool body of water to swim: at first it feels painfully cold and you don't want to make that transition—you'd rather just get out. But if you persevere, you soon get used to it and find the swim wonderfully exhilarating and refreshing. Similarly, you'll be surprised at how potent a few minutes of good meditation can be in the midst of troubles, restoring your awareness of deep joy and lending strength for the struggle. You may learn that a good meditation or good deep prayer is easily possible even under trying circumstances.

In jealousy there is more self-love than love.

—La Rochefoucauld

Entering into Joy

Here are some lines from a remarkable poem, "Matins," by Denise Levertov:

That's joy, it's always
a recognition, the known
appearing fully itself, and
more itself than one knew...

Marvelous Truth confronts us
at every turn
in every guise.

Dwell
in our crowded hearts
our steaming bathrooms, kitchens full of
things to be done, the
ordinary streets.

Thrust close your smile
that we know you, terrible joy.

Can you write something similar out of your deepest and most secret everyday joy?

Chapter Eleven

Living Fully in the Moment

JOY REQUIRES THAT WE not retreat from living life fully and intensely, but bring depth to all our activities. Whatever you do, "do with all your might." Like Jesus, become engaged with the reality of every person and every situation you encounter. Feel the person's pain, share his or her joys, empathize with the pressures and paradoxes of every human situation. Your eyes soften when you see Nancy in obvious pain; they brighten when Joe comes home smiling from a successful first day on his new job; you note the barely concealed tension in Mark and Margaret's living room as they try to pretend you didn't drop in at the wrong time. This responsiveness comes not because you love butting into other people's private soap operas, but because real joyous compassion is terribly *precise*. It is not the fuzzy self-congratulatory good will some may mistake it for, but being truly, totally *aware* of other people. God's love, we are told, numbers the hairs of our heads; our love can at least know all the nuances of glances and smiles. But only caring love can bring you to those nuances so that you see them for what they are. Caring love will also tell you what to do.

It is mostly in little things, encountered on the edges of daily life, that we see visions and miracles, provided we have the clarity to perceive them. But it is in those moments that we know real life beyond mere existence. As Henry David Thoreau said, "To be awake is to be alive," and he added, "I have never yet met a man who was quite awake. How could I have looked him in the face?"

I went to the woods because I wished to live deliberately . . . and not, when I came to die, discover that I had not lived.

—Thoreau

In real engagement with life, the seeds of joy are always there, for engagement means looking outward rather than toward the self. It is paying attention to the realities of the world rather than massaging your own ego. When you are dealing with real problems, worry and anxiety can naturally be present. But so also can the joy of wrestling with them, figuring them out, and either solving them or learning to live with them. Either way is a resolution.

When we hold back from resolving problems or from engaging them or sometimes even from seeing them in the first place, we do not find real joy. At best we only give ourselves an anesthetic, which indeed dulls pain—but also dampens joy. We just go through the motions of life.

Living Fully in the Moment

Opening to deep joy means opening to all of life and therefore to the risk of pain—and to the possibility of finding joy even in pain. For there can be a kind of joy in pain—whether physical or mental—deeper than the pain, yet abiding with it. We can find it if we can find the courage to recognize joy in all intensity of feeling, for feeling intensely is being truly alive, and joy is life. We can find it if we can find in pain just what pain is, a *sharpness* in being alive as part of the universe.

This contention may seem strange, even perverse, but it is not. I am not talking about masochism or the languorous pleasures of some valetudinarian who constantly thinks he's in poor health and loves to have people fuss over him. I am thinking of normal people who know what it means to feel great and aren't always taking their temperatures, but who are like runners who love running even when chest and lungs and shanks ache excruciatingly over the last fifty yards. These people love life even when its cost in pain comes due. They love the way even the pain reminds them they're alive and in the universe, aware of everything, missing nothing, from the severest pain to the most sublime joy.

You also can play some interesting games with pain, whether it's a toothache or a deep-seated anxiety. You will find that you can make the pain come and go depending on the attention you give it. For a time it may seem (horrible to contemplate) the most basic reality of your life. Then you get fully distracted by something else—a book, a TV show, a phone call, a lovely bird song—and poof! for a few moments at least, it's gone. Unless you are really healed, the pain will come back again; I am not talking

He is to learn a diviner art that will . . . turn scorpions into fishes, weeds into flowers, bruises into ornaments, poisons into cordials.
—Thomas Traherne

No athlete is crowned but in the sweat of his brow.
—St. Jerome

about miracle cures. But I am saying that pain is not a constant. It comes and goes with the flow of your mind toward or away from it. Finally, *you* are in control and not the pain; your mind doesn't have to be only reactive but can go where it really wants.

Live here and now, in the present moment. Remember that deep joy is *now;* pain is mostly past and future. A flash of pain in the present instant is nothing, only a flash. What really binds us up with anxious feeling or drags us down with depression is memory of past pain triggered by the present event and anticipation of future pain stemming from it.

Past and future are not real. They are only constructions of mind. True, the mind may use certain memories as building blocks to reconstruct the past and to fashion the future. Still, what we are in the present really determines how we read past and future. If we are anxious and depressed, we will tend to drag up unpleasant and crazy-making memories from the storehouse of the past and build a future out of the darkest present trends in our lives. If we are full of deep joy in the present, we will make a past out of happy memories or of crises from which we emerged triumphant. We will look forward to a future in which everything that is now going well only grows in power.

In the webworks of time, it is easy to get trapped in some tangle or other, unable to get out of a particular occurrence—or imagined future occurrence—and the reactions that go with it. But we must remember that karma is time and time is karma; enlightenment is the timeless now. We can never be enlightened at any other moment than the

Some human beings think the way a spider spins a web. They cannot find the centre of their thoughts. They cannot concentrate their thought to one spot.

—*Sokei-an*

present. Therefore nothing is simpler, on the deepest level, than being enlightened; it is just being here now, fully and completely, without projecting into the future or being weighed down by chains of causation clanking out of the past. It is just being present and awake now.

Bear in mind that past and future are not really what you think them to be. Your past was not really the way you remember it, and your future will not really be the way you now anticipate it, except in broadest outline. No one, unless (as Buddhists would say) a totally enlightened being, has total recall of the past or total clairvoyance toward the future.

The past we remember is really a story we tell ourselves, pegged to a few symbolic incidents, to explain who we now are—or think we are. The future is just a continuation of the same story seen from the often fog-bound perspective of the present.

Consider how little of our past most of us really remember. How much can you actually reconstruct from memory of what you were doing a month ago or even a week ago? Why is it that, when you accidentally come across old letters, journals, or papers you wrote years and years ago, they seem odd to you and yet reveal aspects of your life you had completely put out of mind—and probably will again?

Or think back to when you were, say, eight years old. How much do you actually remember from that year? If you are like most people, probably only two or three clearly defined incidents—a day in school, a trip to the beach, maybe a particularly terrifying experience. Why do you

I shall pass even beyond this power of mind called memory, I shall pass beyond it that I may draw near to you, sweet Light.

—*St. Augustine*

It's a poor sort of
memory that only
works backwards.
—Lewis Carroll

remember just those three out of 365 mostly ordinary days? Undoubtedly because they are convenient representative episodes to fit into the story you tell yourself about who you are today. Other episodes, which may have seemed far more important at the time, are lost to conscious memory because they don't mesh with that story—which is why you feel so funny when an old letter or clipping forces you to recall them again.

The point is that we have largely made our own pasts, working back from the present. So if we say we have to be anxious or depressed or unhappy *now* because of the past, our argument is really circular. It is our *present* unhappiness that leads us to recall that kind of past in the first place. The same goes for seeing trouble in the future.

So the thing to do is to clean up the present moment, fill it with joy, and let its sunshine dissipate the clouds of past and future. This does not mean that any bad thing that objectively did happen or will happen is magically made nonexistent. But their power to hurt will be gone. They will just be there, but impotent, like paper tigers. Let the past be past and the future be future—abstractions both. *You* and deep joy are in the present.

Alcoholics Anonymous advises its members to stay sober just one day at a time. On the same principle, don't worry about ten years or even ten minutes from now. Stay in touch with deep joy here and now, in the present, one second at a time. Nothing can destroy it so quickly as not allowing yourself even the present second of joy! Grief, heavy problems, and physical pain are real, but they depend on tight bondage to past and future for their reality.

If you cut that bond by being in the present, you will find yourself far better able to handle whatever needs to be done about them now—you're always more capable working from joy than from anxiety or distress.

Entering into Joy

1) Try this: Just stop what you're doing for thirty seconds—at work, in the kitchen, or with the children—and realize that you're happy, even though you didn't know it until now.

2) If loving someone in your past is difficult, try this: Think of someone you dearly love now. Experience that love, then let it expand to include others—more and more of them—until finally even the unlovely and seemingly unlovable are brought into the aura of love. (Remember, the unlovable need love the most, and there is virtually no one for whom love cannot be healing—even if conveyed from a distance and only on the inner planes.)

Work until the pain of the relationship is healed and the joyous part of the memory remains strong.

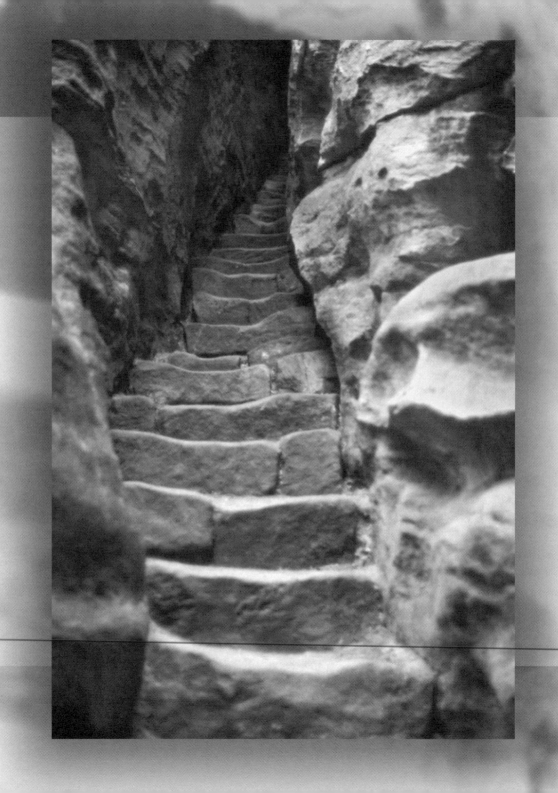

Chapter Twelve

Transcending Obstacles

$\mathcal{A}$FFIRM THE GOOD THAT IS. This is the key to reconciling full engagement with life—accepting its whole emotional tapestry because you are really involved with the world and its people—*and* maintaining deep joy.

When Jesus wept for the death of Lazarus or felt compassion for the sick persons he healed, he was not only expressing his own loss or distress, he was also affirming the good in those people. Something in their lives, he was saying, was worth recovery of life or restoration to fullness of health. In any situation, there is some good. In the most depraved person, some spark of light must remain. In the most hopeless and heartless situation, even a concentration camp, some opportunity for good remains, if only, as for Betsie ten Boom, the opportunity to love and undergo a purifying ordeal.

Seeing and affirming the good may be a matter of perceiving that evil is a matter of scale, as we observed earlier. Though on the personal level you may be having a bad time, the cells and molecules throughout your system may still be sparkling with joy and the earth on which you stand may be dancing with joy as it promenades around the sun.

We are healed of a suffering only by experiencing it to the full.
—Marcel Proust

Joy in Suffering

Difficulties are opportunities. A stormy passage with another person, a parent or spouse, may be a chance to build a new and deeper relationship based on better understanding. Or, if this relationship is genuinely hopeless—which unfortunately is sometimes the case—it may be an occasion for you to grow by realizing that you do not have to be bound forever to a hopeless relationship. You can make the decision to take charge of your life, cut what chains have to be cut, and open yourself to new relationships and new centers of meaning.

Most importantly, the bad times can aid you in learning compassion. When you suffer in mind or body, the road forks. You can go the route of feeling sorry for yourself, dwelling on your pain and the unfairness of life, and sinking further and further into the black hole of self-pity. Or you can determine to let this experience open you to learning more about life in all its dimensions. One of those dimensions, of course, is suffering, no stranger to most of us at one time or another, and a constant companion of many. Your suffering can help you to "feel with" others, which is what *compassion* literally means.

To share another's suffering is a very big thing in itself. What all who suffer want first is to know that there are those—even one—who know about it, share it either actually or in spirit, and deeply care. Some suffering cannot be stopped until either time or death does its work. In these cases, sharing is all that can be done, and it will suffice. Needless to say, it is the nature of compassion and caring to do all that is humanly possible to change the situation so that happiness rather than suffering is what is shared.

All this can be wrought on the forge of your own suffering. Just as colors are hard to explain to one who is blind, so joy is hard to appreciate fully, except against the backdrop of a full spectrum of human experience. Suffering deepens joy even as deep joy dilutes suffering, and nothing deepens joy like compassion. As we have already seen, compassion, love, and joy are closely related because they all articulate the oneness of the universe. Love struggles for unity, joy sings out the even deeper truth that unity is already present. On the human level, both are true and necessary. A wise writer said, "Life itself has speech and is never silent. And its utterance is not, as you that are deaf may suppose, a cry; it is a song."[16]

Finally, suffering can lend us flexibility. Suffering is always an indicator that some change is needed: a different

Knowledge by suffering entereth,
And life is perfected by death.
—*Elizabeth Barrett Browning*

attitude toward a person or situation, a different way of life that reduces stress or augments productivity, a time of rest and recuperation, even a quiet recognition that this particular human existence is coming to an end.

I have spoken of the brittle, dead wood that can only be broken, not bent, and the flexible wood of the sapling that can be pulled to the ground yet spring up again. When suffering tells us something must and will change, we need to consider how we are going to accommodate it: by being broken, shattered to pieces, or by being flexible like the sapling or like water running merrily downhill toward the sea, swirling around or over barriers, in time wearing away the hardest rock, until it reaches its true level.

There are those who think that to be flexible means to be wishy-washy, to lack backbone, to have no principles. But isn't it a matter of *which* principles have priority? A boulder that will not move and can only be dynamited out of the way certainly is not wishy-washy, nor is it doing itself or anyone else any good. A corpse is firm and rigid, but we do not admire it more than we do a living person. If what we affirm is life, then we must affirm life's basic principle, which is that to live is to change, to be supple, to be always ready, both as a species and as individuals, to adapt to new circumstances in the way that best lets life go on as happily as possible. Applied to the self, this means living so that deep joy can arise; applied to a species, it means love by all for all.

For us, then, as for Jesus, our first principles are oneness, joy, and love, both inward and outward. ("Love the Lord your God . . . and your neighbor as yourself.") What serves these principles comes first. As for the rest, we will

We ourselves in the past are not we ourselves now.
—Hsiang-Kuo

be flexible, wise as serpents, and gentle as doves. We will bend in joy at the rapturous wind of the storm and bounce calmly back afterward.

Accepting Limitations

A related matter is the joy of finding freedom in limits. We can learn to appreciate the inner freedom that discovering and accepting limitations to human power can entail. Some discover and must accept that they are partially or totally incapacitated in one or another way: the lame, blind, deaf, those confined to bed. (These are relative matters: all of us have some limitations to seeing and hearing; all of us are confined to bed some of the time.)

For every limit there is a potential compensation. Those with physical or sensory limitations are not disabled, they are differently abled. Those without seeing are able to pick up signals through hearing and touch that escape most of us. Those without hearing can read lips and signs in a way far beyond the rest. Those in wheelchairs can often go farther faster than others can walk or even run.

Some people who have come up against a limit have discovered that acceptance of it is strangely liberating. People with limitations can develop other powers, explore other areas of human experience for which most of us don't have the time or interest—and in this exploration find deep joy.

The greatest compensation is that with less outside stimulation, or (if we are restricted in movement) with less

The main cause of pain lies in our perpetually seeking the permanent in the impermanent.
—H. P. Blavatsky

Insights come and go, but to have them stay, we have to flow with them; otherwise, no change is possible.
—Bernadette Roberts

activity to distract us, we can develop inner worlds. We can pray and meditate more. We can know more of our inner subtle states of consciousness. We can think and understand. We can love those who come to us, and we can delight in deep joy.

All this comes from choosing the right fork in the road.

Death and Rebirth

From the deep-joy perspective, trouble is opportunity. Put another way, it opens initiatory doorways. An initiation is an experience that affects us so deeply and powerfully as to force a realignment of our key symbols, our values, our whole way of being in the universe. Sometimes initiations are programmed for this purpose: the initiations of young people in many societies or initiations into religious mysteries or fraternal organizations come to mind. Even the process of psychotherapy can often be an initiatory passage. At other times, natural occurrences serve as initiations: sickness, childbirth, mystical experiences.

In any case, initiation can be an ordeal out of which comes great transformation. This is why it has often been interpreted in the language of death and rebirth. It is like dying to one life and being reborn as another person, able now to correct what might have gone wrong after the first birth, the physical birth. The symbolization of death and birth in many traditional initiations is very explicit: candidates are semiburied in the ground or enter tomblike chambers, and when they come out they

Setting out on the voyage to Ithaca you must pray that the way be long, full of adventures and experiences.
—*Constantine Peter Cavafy*

It is the old initiates, the spiritual masters, who make [God]. But these masters apply what was revealed to them at the beginning of Time by the Supernatural Beings.
—*Mircea Eliade*

are supposed to stammer and eat soft foods, like new-born babes.

All human lives are really series of initiations. Whether through intent or happenstance, we continually die to one kind of life and are reborn to another. We die to childhood and are born as adults. We die to the delights of simplicity when we enter the education system and, often quite painfully, are reborn as persons of learning. We die to singleness and are reborn to marriage, then to parenthood. And so it goes.

All these rebirths are like the first birth in that they bring us into an unfamiliar world; in each we have to learn to walk, first with only stumbling steps, and we have to learn a language. When we finally master each stage, it is time for another initiation. All persons we meet or know—friends, lovers, teachers, or children—can be our initiators into the shrine of the wide world, even as special and formal initiators can be in esoteric inner chambers of that shrine.

Sickness, suffering, pain, and loss can be the vehicles of these further initiations. Death itself, as was birth, is only another initiation. Life as we know it is a series of initiations: what may seem to be endings are only periods of waiting in the antechamber of the next temple.

We must not expect final rest in the present cycle of our infinite pilgrimage. Rather, we can look at life's ordeals as initiations moving us ahead, teaching us, opening us to wisdom and compassion, helping us explore unexplored worlds, inner and outer. Then we will engage life as it must be engaged, with joy and a shout of victory.

[The initiate] . . . is the twice-born: he has become himself the father.
—*Joseph Campbell*

— *Entering into Joy* —

1) Think about the major transitions in your life, such as adolescence, marriage, the birth of children, or perhaps divorce, the loss of a job, a loved one's death, or a time when you were seriously ill. At each stage, what part of you had to "die" in order for you to become a new person? Beyond the loss, what have you gained? Can you, in retrospect, see an opportunity in the ordeal that was not apparent at the time? Are you in a difficult transition now? If so, what might the opportunity be in it?

2) Reflect on the last time you visited friends in their home. Think about your conversation and the outward things that people did. With love and nonjudgmental compassion, also think about what you saw or heard behind outward appearances. What clues can you find about the troubles from which the people you were with might be suffering? How do their problems mirror your own? End your reflection with a prayer for them . . . and for yourself.

3) Here is a student account:

I woke up to my usual Saturday morning of watching TV and eating breakfast around noon. On this particular day, I felt the need to go into my backyard. I went outside and sat on our brick steps and looked up at the blue sky (not a cloud in sight) and felt the warm sun surround me. It was as though the people in my life who had died had come and surrounded me with love. The sky and the sun engulfed my body with peace and love. I knew at that moment that God was there and that he loved me.

Transcending Obstacles

Think of your deceased loved ones. Pray and meditate for and with them. Let their higher selves—the God within each of them—be like the surrounding love of God for you. Think of the transition they have gone through and prepare yourself for the same transition.

Chapter Thirteen

Finding Deep Joy Today

D EEP DEATHLESS JOY IS THE INNERMOST REALITY of the universe and of ourselves as sons and daughters of that universe, its gods in the making. Joy is our heritage, and we can claim it today.

Some may hold that a gift as exalted as deep joy cannot be forced or claimed; it can come only on its own when the time is right. But this idea represents, I think, a far more passive attitude toward life than we need have. Joy is ours by right and we are empowered to take charge of our lives. Eternity's gifts belong to any and all points in time. The teachings of all religions regarding prayer and meditation indicate that we are to lay hold of divine gifts, not to insult heaven by scorning them.

You can start today, then, to reach for the gift of deep joy. Sit down and think about your life. When do you know joy, and what seems to block it at other times? First, the negatives. What can be done about the blockages? Should you make any change in your attitude, in your lifestyle, in what you are doing with your life?

Even more importantly, think about the positives, the places in your life where seeds of deep joy are already planted. Whether they are in the jubilant way you respond to nature, to sports, to children, to your present religion, or even to the challenges of work doesn't matter; they represent sources of growth toward greater joy that you can nourish. They can spark your spiritual Awakening. Cultivate those seeds, and from them let grow the vine of the spiritual way and the fruit of union with universal joy.

But remember that the Awakening stage is a roller coaster. Before long, the euphoria of that first level, probably emotional, will wear off. It is very important that at the right moment you transfer the deep joy from nature or sports or whatever your passion is to a regularly structured spiritual life—in other words, to regular prayer or meditation. In this way you learn to engage the process directly, and you do it whether you feel like it or not. At the same time, look again at your lifestyle and see whether it is consistent with your general values or whether some realignment is in order.

From the remotest antiquity, mankind as a whole have always been convinced of the existence of a personal spiritual entity within the personal physical man.
—H. P. Blavatsky

The unexamined life is not worth living.
—Plato

Finding Deep Joy Today

In time, you may know deep joy on the wonderful level of Illumination. Afterward, if your wisdom deepens with your joy and you learn to let nothing get you down, the passage of the Dark Night of the Soul will take care of itself, and Union will free you to know the deepest secret of the universe, joy.

I am the vine;
you are the branches.
If a man remains in me
and I in him, he will
bear much fruit.
—Jesus, John 15:5

Notes

1. Citations of the Upanishads are from Swami Prabhanvananda and Frederick Manchester, trans., *The Upanishads: Breath of the Eternal.* © The Vedanta Society of Southern California, 1948. Reprinted by permission.

2. J. C. Chatterji, *The Wisdom of the Vedas.* Wheaton, IL: Theosophical Publishing House, 1973, p. 25.

3. Quotations from Job in the text are from *The New English Bible.* © The Delegates of the Oxford University Press and The Syndics of the Cambridge Press, 1961, 1970. Reprinted by permission. Those in the margin are from *The New Oxford Annotated Bible.* New York: Oxford University Press, 1991, 1994.

4. Thomas Byron, trans. *The Dhammapada: The Sayings of the Buddha.* New York: Random House Vintage Books, 1976, pp. 75, 76. © Alfred A. Knopf, Inc. Reprinted by permission.

5. William Shakespeare, *As You Like It*, Act II, Scene 7.

6. William Shakespeare, *The Tempest*, Act IV, Scene 1.

7. Margaret Smith, *Rabi'a the Mystic.* Cambridge University Press, 1928, p. 99. Reprinted by permission.

8. Smith, p. 30.

9. Ibid., p. 27.

10. Paul Reps, *Zen Flesh, Zen Bones.* Garden City: Doubleday Anchor Books, p. 154. Originally published in Nyogen Senzaki, *10 Bulls*, trans. by Paul Reps. Los Angeles: DeVorss and Company, 1935.

11. Valentine Zander, *St. Seraphim of Sarov.* London: SPCK, 1975, pp. 79–80. Reprinted by permission.

12. Zander, p. 90.

13. Jan van Ruysbroeck, *The Adornment of the Spiritual Marriage.* C. A. Wynschenck, trans. London: J. M. Dent and Sons, 1916, pp. 169–70.

14. Details of how to meditate effectively using various techniques are discussed in the companion book to this one, *Finding the Quiet Mind.* Wheaton, IL: Theosophical Publishing House, Quest Books, 1983.

15. Corrie ten Boom, *The Hiding Place.* Lincoln, VA: Chosen Books, 1971.

16. Mabel Collins, *Light on the Path.* Wheaton, IL: Theosophical Publishing House [1885], 1970, p. 26.

The poem on p. 119 by Denise Levertov is from *Poems 1960–1967*, copyright © 1966 by Denise Levertov. Reprinted by permission of New Directions Publishing Corp.

QUEST BOOKS

are published by

The Theosophical Society in America,

Wheaton, Illinois 60189-0270,

a branch of a world fellowship,

a membership organization

dedicated to the promotion of the unity of

humanity and the encouragement of the study of

religion, philosophy, and science, to the end that

we may better understand ourselves and our place in

the universe. The Society stands for complete

freedom of individual search and belief.

For further information about its activities,

write, call 1-800-669-1571, e-mail olcott@theosmail.net

or consult its Web page: http://www.theosophical.org

The Theosophical Publishing House

is aided by the generous support of

THE KERN FOUNDATION,

a trust established by Herbert A. Kern

and dedicated to Theosophical education.